D1187820

INDIA
The Future
is Now

EDITED BY
SHASHI THAROOR

INDIA

The Future is Now

**THE VISION AND
ROAD MAP FOR
THE COUNTRY
BY HER YOUNG
PARLIAMENTARIANS**

wisdom
tree

cartoons by **Sudhir Tailang**

INDIA

Text and photograph: Respective contributors
Cartoons: Sudhir Tailang
Conceptualisation: Shobit Arya
© Wisdom Tree

First published 2013

ISBN 978-81-8328-296-3

Published by

Wisdom Tree
4779/23, Ansari Road
Darya Ganj, New Delhi-110002
Ph.: 011-23247966/67/68
wisdomtreebooks@gmail.com

Printed in India

Contents

Sorry, you can't enter unless you show
the proof that you're above 70!

Young Leadership and the Future of India

SHASHI THAROOR

The young parliamentarians who have authored the dozen essays in this book have taken on a broad sweep of the nation's problems. Anantkumar Hegde discusses agriculture, education and the environment. Anurag Singh Thakur focuses on national security. Hamdullah Sayeed, the youngest of the lot, concentrates entirely on education. Jay Panda, amongst the oldest, discusses economic growth (including the inevitable comparisons with China), education and caste politics. Jyotiraditya Scindia's emphasis is on inclusive growth, with special reference to agriculture, education and social justice. Kalikesh Narayan Singh Deo discusses hunger, corruption and political change, particularly welcoming the role of regional parties. MB Rajesh offers a critique of economic reforms and suggests an alternative approach to addressing urgent problems of inequality. Milind Deora examines development at a time of rapid urbanisation. Nishikant Dubey seeks to bridge the urban-rural divide, particularly in skills, health and tourism. Poonamben Jat covers corruption, agriculture, education, human development and women's empowerment. Priya Dutt Roncon discusses education, health and the welfare of women and children. And Sanjay Jaiswal examines manufacturing, health and clean energy.

This is an impressive list, and it points to the urgent concern with India's compelling problems that animates young Indian leaders across the country's political divides. The contributors span the spectrum from left to right, represent both the Government and the Opposition and hail from both rural and urban constituencies. Their essays offer a good idea of the range and breadth of what young Indians with an eye on the future believe matters, as they navigate their way through the national political minefield.

For India's challenges are considerable, and there's a reason why we're still 'emerging', rather than, as President Obama so flatteringly put it in his November 2010 address to Parliament, already 'emerged'. Our teeming cities overflow, while two out of three Indians still scratch a living from the soil. We have been recognised, for all practical purposes, as a leading nuclear power, but 400 million Indians still have no access to electricity and there are daily power cuts even in the nation's capital. We are the world's leading manufacturers of generic medication for illnesses such as AIDS, but we have 2.3 million people living with HIV-AIDS, another two million with tuberculosis and tens of millions with no health centre or clinic within ten kilometres of their places of residence. India holds both the world record for the number of cell phones sold, and also for the number of farmer suicides (an estimated 15,000 per year, because when harvests fail, farmers are crushed by a crippling mountain of debt and feel the only way out is to take their own lives).

And, as we all know, inflation, particularly of food and fuel prices, lurid stories of corruption and rising interest rates are causing concern to investors and have prompted some to see India less as an 'emerging market' than as a 'submerging polity'. There is no room for complacency.

Where do young political leaders in India fit into this uncertain future?

India is a remarkably young country. The nation's average age is 28; indeed, 66 per cent of the population is under 35, which means that the young are already a majority in India. But they are not the ruling majority, according to *The Economist*, India holds the world record for the largest gap between the average age of the population and that of the Cabinet (which is 65). The young are entering leadership positions, but still with diffidence—and they continue to be outnumbered by their seniors.

And yet India's youth population could be an asset unlike any other. We have a great demographic advantage in 600 million young people under 25, which means we should have a dynamic, youthful and productive workforce for the next forty years when the rest of the world is ageing. But we also have 60 million child labourers, and 56 per cent of the children in our government schools drop out by the eighth standard. We have trained world-class scientists and engineers, but 350 million of our compatriots are illiterate, and we also have more children who have not seen the inside of a school than any other country in the world does. We celebrate India's IT triumphs, but information technology has employed a grand total of 5 million people in the last twenty years, while 10 million are entering the workforce each year and we don't have jobs for them. Many of our urban youth rightly say with confidence that their future will be better than their parents' past, but there are Maoist insurgencies violently disturbing the peace in 165 of India's 629 districts, and these are largely made up of unemployed young men.

The Government of India is conscious of the need for rapid change. As a freshly-elected Member of Parliament myself in 2009, I recall Prime Minister Manmohan Singh, then 78, urging us to always respect 'the impatience of the young'. India's under-35s are a generation that holds our nation to new, higher standards befitting the globalised era, standards that they understand prevail in the developed world. They are a generation born in the era of liberalisation, growing up with greater freedoms, more choices and opportunities than their forebears, impatient with the heavy hand of government and tired of shopworn rhetoric about socialism and upliftment of the masses. They want action, not slogans; results, not bromides.

And yet there is a significant gap between the political process and the participation in it of India's brightest young sons and daughters. This is a separation which is intolerable and one which can be ignored only at our own peril—both at the individual level and at the level of the nation. It was not so at the time of the freedom struggle, when the best and most energetic minds, cutting across all professional classes, actively participated in the political process of the nationalist movement. After the first flush of independence, though, that enthusiasm has been replaced by indifference. The middle-class, educated young turn to the professions, to civil service exams and to multinational corporations, yet few amongst them spare a thought for politics.

But change is in the air. More educated young people are beginning to think the previously unthinkable and contemplate a political career.

It is true that the majority of young parliamentarians hail from political families. Many of this book's authors have politics in their blood: most have had illustrious political fathers, and one is a third-generation politician. Only three climbed up the party worker route to being nominated to contest elections, and just two (Panda and Dubey) gave up completely different careers (in the corporate world) to bring their talents to politics. They may, however, mark the start of a trend. The days when smart, educated people like the writers of this volume stay away from politics are disappearing. More and more young persons are convinced that they cannot afford to be 'apolitical' any more. There is too much at stake.

Young people keeping away from politics will only restrict the progress and growth of our country in the twenty-first century. Staying aloof is a personal choice, but it is also an abdication of responsibility. The founding fathers of this nation believed passionately that multiparty democracy was the most suitable system for a nation of such richness in diversity and dynamic potential as India. They have left behind a legacy that the young generation has begun to realise it cannot squander.

Three years ago I wrote a letter to young professionals in my constituency, urging them to get involved in politics. I argued: 'Politics is not merely about elections every few years. It is about determining the choices your country makes, which intimately affect your daily lives wherever you live and work. Our government is doing a great deal that young people can't afford to be indifferent to. Decisions are being taken on life and death issues about yourself and your families—and if you are not involved in the process that arrives at those decisions, it simply means that you do not care. Vital decisions that will affect your professional opportunities, the investment climate in our country, the way in which revenues are raised and spent, and the policies that will affect your own advancement, are being formulated and taken in various forums—by local bodies, the state legislature and at the national level through our Parliament. It's the political process that establishes these institutions and determines their composition. Please join it.'

The response was modest, but the young have begun to stir. Many have turned out in the streets to voice their concerns, whether about corruption or other urgent social wrongs, most recently about the brutal gang-rape of a twenty-three-year-old woman in Delhi. The challenge is to channel their energy into constructive political action.

The ruling party has already understood the need to nurture in the young generation a strong, vibrant and visionary leadership totally rooted in the Indian ethos of democracy. It has actively encouraged the democratisation of governance and the active participation of the citizenry in governance, right from the grass-roots level. Path-breaking legislation, such as creating and strengthening the Panchayati Raj institutions, establishing the Mahatma Gandhi Rural Employment Guarantee Scheme and promulgating the Right to Information Act, are examples of innovative policies inspired and enacted in recent years that have created conducive ground for mass political mobilisation.

Few Indian parties, however, have moved rapidly enough with the times. Only one—my own—has begun to put in place compulsory elections to party posts, starting from the grass-roots level. Instead of leaders being thrust on them from above, young people want to elect their own party leaders. It is this desire to ensure fairness and promote true representativeness which will ensure that a party remains true to its democratic roots and remains a potent force in the political fabric of the nation.

***

It has become a cliché to speak of India as a land of paradoxes. The old joke about our country is that anything you say about India, the opposite is also true. We like to think of ourselves as an ancient civilisation but we are also a young republic; our IT experts stride confidently into the twenty-first century but much of our population seems to live in each of the other twenty centuries. Quite often, the opposites coexist quite cheerfully. One of my favourite images of India is from the last Kumbh Mela, of a naked sadhu, straight out of central casting, with matted hair, ash-smeared forehead and scraggly beard, a *rudraksha* mala around his scrawny neck and a distant gaze in his eyes, for all the world a picture of timeless other-worldliness, chatting away on a mobile phone.

Young Indians are growing into such a paradoxical India. What are the prospects for the expansion of the participative political space in tomorrow's India, say over the next two decades? To me this desirable objective requires both growth and equity. It is happening, but there's still a lot that needs to be done before we get there.

The benefits of economic growth must reach all Indians—the majority of whom are young, and the majority of whom are poor. Statisticians tell us that the current proportion of the total Indian population under 25 years of age is 51 per cent and the proportion under 35 is about 66 per cent. This predominance of youth in the population is expected to last until 2050, with the average age of an Indian in 2020 expected to be 29 years.

This is both good news and bad news. The good news is that this means we will have a productive, dynamic, even youthful working-age population for decades, while most of the planet, including China, is ageing. (China's current average age is 38; in ten years, it will be 50). We used to bemoan our failures at population control, especially in contrast to China; but when one single Chinese, born from his country's one-child policy, is desperately trying to support four grandparents, his Indian counterpart, the child of our country's population-control failures, will be riding the cusp of a demographic boom. In the next twenty years, the labour force in China will shrink by 5 per cent, and in the industrialised 'Northern' world, by 4 per cent; in the same time frame, India's labour force will increase by 32 per cent.

But then, there's the bad news. The availability of a human resource of such magnitude only means anything if we can feed, house, clothe, educate and train these young people so they can actually contribute to socio-economic change. If we fail to provide them the opportunities to make something of their lives in the new India, the same population could be not only a burden but even a threat, since so much of terrorism and extremist violence in our country is carried out by embittered and unemployed young men.

How are we going to give them these opportunities? Plainly not through agriculture alone, because rural India already cannot sustain the 600 million people currently trying to live off the land. That is why India is suffering the painful tragedy of farmer suicides every time the monsoon disappoints and the harvests fail to sustain a debt-ridden farmer's family. Over the next two decades, India will witness a massive migration from the rural areas to the urban, both to existing cities and towns and through the transformation of rural centres into urban townships.

In turn this will have an impact on other vital aspects of Indian life. First, on our education system, which will have to cope with hundreds of millions of young people who no longer intend to be farmers and peasants, but will want the education that will equip them to lead viable urban lives. Second, on our demand for and consumption of energy, which will multiply exponentially as new infrastructure is built and as urban dwellers seek electricity, water, drainage, roads, telephone connections and mass transit. Today, 400 million Indians, overwhelmingly in rural areas, are not even connected to the electricity grid. Tomorrow they will be. Our government aims to increase power generation in India by seven times—700 per cent—over the next 25 years.

If, say, 300 million Indians were to move from the villages to the towns in the next two decades or less, can we absorb all of them, educate all of them, employ all of them? If India succeeds in accommodating and absorbing these young people, we can enhance their life chances by enabling them to seize the opportunities of the twenty-first century. This is a task that must be taken on by a society that in 2009 passed a Right to Education Act, embracing all children everywhere in our country. Right now, desperately poor parents in India, working as rickshaw-pullers and domestic servants, are scrimping and saving to send their children to mediocre private schools that they can ill afford, because they see a decent education in English as the best guarantee of their child's future. Now the state is stepping in to ensure that their dreams do not have to constitute an impossible burden on them.

If that works, and we bring the benefits of education to every illiterate child in India today, then perhaps 200 million of the 300 million people I spoke about will suddenly be able to compete with the rest of the world. I say to Westerners: these Indians tomorrow will be able to answer your phones, make your airline reservations and pursue your credit-card defaulters, but they will also be able to read your MRIs, design your automobiles, write your legal briefs and invent your next gadgets.

That's if we succeed. What if we fail? As a political representative in India today, I certainly do not take the prospects of success for granted. The process of doing what I have described is not just huge in itself, it also involves something no society, not even China, has yet attempted. And that is to connect millions of citizens in a functioning democracy to their own government: not just to announce entitlements that will be showered upon them by a munificent government, but to provide opportunities that they are expected to grasp for themselves, and to create delivery mechanisms that ensure that these opportunities and entitlements are not just theoretical, but real and accessible.

This is essential in all societies, but it is indispensable in a democracy. As a Member of Parliament, I am struck by the fact that a majority of the voters in every Indian constituency are, by international standards, poor. The basics—food, clothing, shelter, roads, electricity, drinking water, jobs—dominate our politics. This is why my party has focussed on inclusive growth—the combination of economic development and social justice—as the lodestar of its work.

If this is important enough when voters are poor, it is deeply significant when they are both poor and young. Young people in India are now asking that their voices be heard, that their issues be addressed and that their roles be recognised. They want to be accepted as partners for development, helping to chart a common course and shaping the future for everyone.

As young India grows into and demands change, our national politics is undergoing a vital shift as well. I believe that a major reason why my party won the 2009 General Elections is that our political leadership was able to delink the national polity from the incendiary issues of religious identity and caste denomination that other parties had built their appeal upon. Instead, we put the focus on what the people needed—more development, better governance, wider socio-economic opportunities.

And yet, paradoxically, the stresses of economic development have created disparities which risk becoming centrifugal forces, dividing our society between rich and poor, urban and rural. To counteract this, we need to devise creative, ambitious responses to deal with the challenges faced by our people—to connect them to the opportunities the twenty-first century offers.

One such response is the Mahatma Gandhi National Rural Employment Guarantee Act (MGNREGA), which provides a hundred days of paid employment as a matter of right to one member of every rural family below the poverty line. Another is the expansion of micro-credit to the rural poor, and a third possible response in the near future will be the Food Security Act my government is currently working on.

The objective of such measures is inclusion and connection—inclusion in the great Indian twenty-first century story, and connection to the institutional structures within which that story unfolds. In my visits to the poor and dispossessed, when I am in Thiruvananthapuram, I am acutely conscious that the opposite is still the reality for millions of my fellow Indians. They face exclusion and disconnection for a variety of reasons: their place in the traditional social structure, their caste, their poverty, but also because our country has not been able to build the physical means—the roads, the highways, the power-transmission lines, the telephone systems, the schools—to connect them. India's most powerful young leader, Rahul Gandhi, rightly speaks of two Indias—one connected, one not. Establishing the connection between the two Indias is vital to our country's place in the world, and vital to developing a convincing sense of a liberal democratic India.

And if we succeed—when we succeed—we will be connecting 500 million Indians, over the next two decades, to their own country and to the rest of the world. Half a billion villagers will join the global village. That is an exciting prospect. But only then can we truly speak of an India ready to fulfil its huge potential.

Yes, we still have huge problems to overcome. Some claim we are a superpower, but we are also super poor. We can't really be both of those. We have to overcome our poverty. We have to deal with the hardware of development—the ports, the roads, the airports, all the infrastructural progress we need to make—and the software of development, the human capital: the need for ordinary people in India to be able to have a couple of square meals a day, to be able to send their children to a decent school, and to aspire to work a job that will give them opportunities in their lives to transform themselves. We are, however fitfully, on course to do all this.

But to play a major role in the twenty-first century—to fulfil its undoubted potential—India also needs to solve its internal problems. We must ensure that we do enough to keep our people healthy, well-fed and secure—secure not just from jihadi terrorism, a real threat, but from the daily terror of poverty, hunger and ill-health. Progress is being made: we can take satisfaction from India's success in carrying out three kinds of revolutions in feeding our people—the 'green revolution' in foodgrains, the 'white revolution' in milk production and, at least to some degree, a 'blue revolution' in the development of our fisheries. But the benefits of these revolutions have not yet reached the third of our population still living below the poverty line.

Our growth was never only about per capita income figures. It was always a means to an end. And the ends we cared about were the uplift of the weakest sections of our society, the expansion of employment possibilities for them, the provision of decent healthcare and clean drinking water. Those ends remain. Whether we grow by 9 per cent, as we once did, or by just about 6 per cent, as we did in 2012, our fundamental commitment must be to the bottom 25 per cent of our society.

But it's all taking place, this great adventure of conquering those challenges, those real challenges which none of us in India can pretend don't exist. And it is all taking place in an open society, in a rich and diverse and plural civilisation, in one that is open to the contention of ideas and interests within it, unafraid of the prowess or the products of the outside world, wedded to the democratic pluralism that is India's greatest strength, and determined to liberate and fulfil the creative energies of its people. That is the transformed India of the early twenty-first century, and its future—and the place of young leadership in that future—is well worth celebrating.

ಶ್ರೀ

Anantkumar Hegde

Elected to the Lok Sabha regularly since 1996 from the Uttara Kannada constituency, Anantkumar Hegde is a leader of the Bharatiya Janata Party.

Born in 1968 to a landed farming family, this four-time Member of Parliament has been politically active on several fronts for more than two decades. His familial association with the land and the people who are sustained by it, has allowed him to take interest in rural development and envision plans for the rejuvenation of the agricultural sector. He has also been a Member of the PSU Committee.

A multifaceted personality, Hegde also runs an NGO, Kadamba, engaged in socio economic upliftment, formation of self-help groups, rural marketing, community education and rural health services. Interestingly, Kadamba also supports research on recovering ancient manuscripts from the countryside.

A classical music buff, Hegde is an enthusiastic advocate of Hindi as the national language. A keen sports lover, he is also trained in tae-kwon-do.

INDIA

Sir, 100s of crores that we spent haven't gone down the drain! We've saved it—that's the river Yamuna!

Sow the Right Seeds, Reap Fortune

Agriculture continues to be the biggest contributor to the country's Gross Domestic Product (GDP). It contributes nearly 16 per cent to the GDP, occupies almost 43 per cent of the country's geographical area and 52 per cent of India's population is associated with this sector.

Six decades ago, when India became an independent nation, there were hopes and dreams. The nation-builders dreamt of a developed, self-reliant country. They worked towards that goal. But somewhere along the way, things didn't quite turn out as expected. The focus got blurred, plans went awry—some things worked, and others didn't. Mistakes were made and rectified; yet, many things just didn't seem to work in favour of the country. The dream of a developed nation was far from being realised. Sixty years on, it still remains to come true. But the last few years have renewed hopes. India is today one of the prominent economies in the world, chugging along confidently on the road to superpowerdom. If the right steps are taken immediately, there is no reason why India can't achieve its dream of becoming a developed nation.

A few sectors are crucial to India's growth, and it is here that we need to take corrective steps. Agriculture, the mainstay of India's economy; education, without which a nation cannot be built and environment, important for a country's longevity—are the sectors which have to see radical improvement.

AGRICULTURE

In recent years, the services sector and industries may have become major players, but agriculture continues to be the biggest contributor to the country's Gross Domestic Product (GDP). By itself, it contributes nearly 14 per cent to the GDP. It occupies almost 43 per cent of the country's geographical area and 52 per cent of India's population is associated with this sector. India is the second largest producer of wheat and rice in the world. It is the largest producer of fruit and vegetables, milk, major spices, millets, castor oil seed, among many others. Yet, a major drawback of Indian agriculture is that it lacks a well-laid-out plan or policy by the government. Farmers are free to grow anything they like, without as much as a thought for the nation or their own welfare. There are virtually no agencies which guide the farmers to grow what is really required and in what quantity.

We should work out a plan which takes into account the need of the country as a whole. Crop planning is essential to achieve optimal productivity, maximum profits and better use of land. I come from a family of agriculturists and, as a result, have been closely associated with crops and land. My village in Uttara Kannada district, which is the western part of Karnataka, is one of the richest in biodiversity. For years we have grown millet, which is the staple food of the villagers. But with the government pushing for cash crops like rice and wheat, which soak up a lot of water, millet farming is gradually disappearing.

In fact, local crops such as bajra, jowar, ragi are being sidelined for rice and wheat, the consumption of which is higher in the urban areas.

It has to be realised that the farmers are better off producing local crops. A report in *The Times of India* (5 June 2012) stated how many farmers in North Karnataka, near Hubli, switched to wheat farming after the government started giving huge fertilizer subsidies. But when the crops started failing due to unpredictable weather, many took to Bt Cotton farming and many others went into debt. Such situations can be prevented if the government emphasizes local crops. Millets, for instance, require low maintenance but have a high yield. Besides, people in parts of India's hinterland still eat local grains. Similarly, local crops should be grown to fulfil the needs of the local region.

How can the yield of the local foodgrain and other crops be increased? For that we need better research. Unfortunately, we are dependent on technology from the US and Europe. So much money is spent on just importing technology; instead, we should develop indigenous technology and carry out research in foodgrains. It is sad that the government is concentrating on things like Bt Brinjal and Bt Cotton, which have reportedly been found to be harmful to both environment and human health. The controversy around Bt Brinjal has caused the government to stop it from being introduced in India. Instead of wasting time and money on brinjals, we should concentrate on producing foodgrains such as millets etc. We can live without Bt Brinjal but it is impossible to live without foodgrains. India has a huge variety of crops; we should focus on developing them.

Let's learn from the consequences that farmers have been facing since the time Bt Cotton was introduced. The government had launched genetically modified cotton ten years ago, in 2002, with the promise that farmers would get miraculous crop yields. A report by Coalition for GM-Free India said that in the period

2011-12, the spate of farmer suicides has been largely among Bt Cotton farmers. When the crops fail, farmers are not able to afford the seeds, leading to despair and helplessness among them. Further, government estimates in December 2011 found that in Andhra Pradesh, of the 47 lakh acres planted with Bt Cotton, nearly 33.73 lakh acres suffered from crop failure.

Our agriculture is entirely dependent on the monsoon. If the monsoon fails, our crops fail and in turn, the farmers suffer. We still don't have a system whereby we can accurately predict the onset of monsoon. With global warming gradually becoming a reality, it is important that we don't depend on growing short-term crops. Let the farmers be educated about growing non-seasonal crops. India has vast tracts of dry, non-irrigable land, which remain largely unusable. These can be used for horticulture or growing agro-fuels. The non-profit organisation that I run, Kadamba, has been involved in various fields, including horticulture. Our sustained efforts in Uttara Kannada in the field of horticulture have seen some positive results. For instance, the horticulture area has increased from 26 to 48 per cent in the last three years and the revenue has gone up to ₹60 crore per annum. If a small organisation can achieve this, I am sure the government can do much better. The benefits of horticulture are many. For instance, in horticulture, usually a long-term crop is grown. This automatically cuts down the dependency on the monsoon every year. Then, it requires less irrigation, thus saving groundwater to a large extent. Further, the monetary returns are much more as compared to agriculture. It also helps in increasing the green cover, therefore making it environmentally viable. It provides more scope for processing industries, leading to an increase in the demand for fruit and vegetables, both fresh and processed. Most importantly, the crop failure risk is minimal. With so many benefits, it only makes sense to promote horticulture in a big way. I would suggest that we develop a fresh model of stepping ahead 'from foodgrain security to nutrition security' for a healthy India, by promoting horticulture. In addition, we should focus on the growth of the horticulture sector through increased participation of small and marginal farmers in an organised manner. Steps are being taken in this sector but a lot still needs to be done.

India imported crude oil worth $160 billion in the first ten months of the financial year 2011-12. This was excluding the crude oil imported for processing and re-export. Every year the crude oil bill keeps increasing, which is definitely not good for the economy. One way of reducing our import bills would be to invest in growing biofuels. India has vast tracts of dry land which can be used to grow biofuels. After all, they are the future. Not only will we save foreign exchange, but our farmers will also become independent and prosperous. In the process, our forest cover area, which according to the India State of Forest Report 2011 is 78.29 million hectares, will grow. What we haven't done in sixty years, can easily be achieved in the next twenty years—of course, if it's done effectively.

EDUCATION

The foundation of a strong and confident nation is its education system. Unless good quality education is provided to all, a nation cannot pride itself on producing great citizens. Centuries ago, before the Mughals and the British conquered India, we had an excellent system of education which emphasized not just learning the arts and sciences but also the culture, values and traditions of the nation. The *gurukul* system of education was widely prevalent. We had world-class centres of learning such as the Nalanda and Taxila universities. We gave the world the zero and produced some of the greatest thinkers, scientists, philosophers and patriots. But over the years, things have changed and anglicised education that is prevalent today has taken the young away from their traditions and roots. To bring back the feeling of pride in one's culture and heritage, it is important that the medium of instruction should be the mother tongue. It is only the mother tongue which can bring us close to our traditions; steeped in emotions and expression, the impact of the mother tongue is such that no other language can have. One's mother tongue is like one's lifeline. Indonesia's first president, Sukarno, had once famously said, 'You can change my name but not my blood.' This holds true of one's mother tongue. But this doesn't mean that the students will not have the opportunity to learn other languages. They can and should learn different languages. But the way the languages are taught matters a lot. The problem with the way we teach languages is that we tend to make them pedantic and grammar-oriented, and as a result, students falter in picking up a language. Rather, introduce the language, not only the grammar.

Our teaching methods need a major overhaul. We are too dependent on rote learning—students learn from a prescribed text blindly and schools focus on results. Value education is rare. Students are rarely encouraged to question or experiment in school. There is no emphasis on practical education. There is no concept of learning through stories. The art of storytelling is literally lost. Children no longer rely on their memory; everything is available at a click. This is why we need to revamp our primary education system. We need to make it more practical, independent of bookish knowledge and oriented to learning one's culture and values.

When it comes to higher education, the number of universities/ university-level institutions has increased 18 times from 27 in 1950 to 620 in 2013. There are 44 central universities, 298 State universities, 148 private universities and 130 deemed universities. The number of colleges has increased from 578 in 1950 to more than 30,000 in 2011. It is good that the number of colleges and universities is increasing but what's sad is that we have no concept of human research mapping. Unlike the western countries, in India we have no idea of our requirements of doctors, engineers, teachers or scientists. The government keeps on introducing new courses and churning out doctors, engineers or arts graduates by the dozen. Most of them end up without jobs or seek opportunities abroad. All our investments in education go waste. With human resource mapping, we can study the requirements and open institutes in accordance with the requirements, and can introduce only those courses which would help the country in the future.

At present, everybody wants to become a software engineer. Interestingly, India has the largest technical and scientific manpower globally. As per a 2011 report of the National Association of Software and Services Companies (Nasscom), the out-turn—the number coming out of colleges—of technical graduates and postgraduates increased to over 700,000 from a little over 550,000 in 2010. In the same year, enrolment in technology colleges increased sharply from 1.2 million to 1.6 million. Interest in other subjects is much less. It's all about earning big money and pursuing a career without actually taking into consideration the student's aptitude and interest. There is a need to have more courses in subjects such as biotechnology. If we want improved quality of food and grains, we have to have experts in the respective fields. And that is possible only when we have the required courses. Nanotechnology, which is so important today, is not taught as an undergraduate course in India. Only recently, the University Grants Commission chairman told me that it will soon be introduced in the undergraduate studies.

We have to remember that technology can change the face of a country. Look at Israel. Sixty years ago, it was a fledgling state. Six decades later, it is one of the most advanced countries in South

West Asia in economic and industrial development. In 2010, as per the International Institute for Management Development (IMD) *World Competitiveness Yearbook*, Israel ranked seventeenth among the world's most economically developed nations. Intensive development in agriculture has made the nation self-sufficient in food production. Further, Israel has led the world in stem-cell research and its universities are among the top 100 world universities in mathematics, physics, chemistry, computer science and economics. India certainly has a lot to learn from Israel.

Coming back to the state of our universities, it has been observed that the emphasis on humanities is getting weaker. Very few today want to pursue a career in the social sciences. Look at the sad state of humanities in the country—only those students take it up who have not got admission into any other technical course. There is no realisation that the study of humanities is as important to the growth of a nation as technical education. We need philosophers, poets, writers and thinkers too. Values need to be inculcated in the young of today. Scientific knowledge should combine itself with a sense of social responsibility and values in building up the national character. And that's when we can produce more leaders like Subhash Chandra Bose and Mahatma Gandhi. We need to revive the interest in humanities and this should be done at the level of tehsil schools. If we don't do this, we will end up producing robots.

It's true that education should translate into gainful employment. But how can we do that if we have no focus on what our students should be reading in colleges and universities? With an unemployment rate of nearly 10 per cent, it is imperative that we identify courses which can help students to get good jobs. Say, for example, a course in carpentry or mobile repairing or even yoga. Do we even know that yoga has a huge worldwide demand? And when we have the knowledge, why can't we train students in this science and send yoga teachers to countries which need them the most? But first we have to identify the courses which can generate employment. Germany, for instance, has identified some 250 courses for higher education. The problem is that we have the potential but we don't know how to exploit it.

In such a scenario, the present government is trying to get foreign institutions to set up base here. The Foreign Educational Institutions (Regulation of Entry and Operations) Bill 2010 has been introduced in Parliament. Now, that is not such a big problem. We can afford to give our students world-class education but what we should remember is that the syllabus should be completely ours. Let the foreign institutions give us their expertise and technology.

A good, practical education is the foundation of a prosperous nation. Education has to be modern yet rooted in tradition and culture. The aim of our colleges and universities has to be to produce independent, thinking, learned individuals who are patriotic. Let's start now, and in a few years we will achieve part of our dream.

ENVIRONMENT

India is rich in biodiversity. It is home to 7 per cent of the recorded species in the world. Nearly 91,200 species of animals and 45,500 types of plants can be found here. Rich mineral deposits can be found across the country. Six major climatic subtypes are found in India. The water surface area accounts for 31,440 km and receives an average annual rainfall of 1,100 mm. Yet, over the years, this vast natural resource has come under threat. Large-scale pollution has impacted our air, water and land. Our main river, the Ganga, is almost dying; our forest cover is depleting, marine life is under threat and the air is almost unbreathable.

The Environment Protection Act 1986 was brought into force to save India's environment. But even after twenty-six years, the Act hasn't really made a great impact. A major lacuna of the Act is a weak enforcement policy. The clause regarding groundwater, for instance, is too vague. The way we are using up the groundwater, in ten years, it'll be depleted. When it comes to rivers, the country's lifelines, there is really no strict punishment for those polluting them. India's fourteen major rivers and several other minor ones receive millions of litres of sewage, industrial and agricultural wastes. Many of them have been reduced to stinking sewage drains. The Ganga, revered by the Hindus down the ages, is today one of the most polluted Indian rivers. A study conducted by the Uttarakhand Environment Conservation and Pollution Control Board says that the Ganga water is not just unfit for drinking or bathing but even unusable for agricultural purposes. What is shocking is that in Varanasi, says the report, the coliform bacterial count is at least 3,000 times higher than the standard established as safe by the World Health Organization. The industries along the course of the river are a major source of pollution. The tanneries in north India are one of the many sources which are responsible for turning the Ganga into a dumping ground. Despite innumerable studies and reports, the government has not been able to take action against these polluting industries. No strict initiative has been taken to stop the industries from releasing pollutants into the river. Unless there is a strict penalty, we may not be able to save the Ganga from dying.

Let's take a cue from what has been done to the Yamuna. It is almost a dead river now. Some 2,000 million litres of sewage, most of it untreated, goes into the river from Delhi alone every day. In spite of the huge amount of money being pumped in to save the river, no changes can be seen. It is our greed and callous attitude that is killing our waterbodies and if we don't take action now, we will be in great trouble in the future.

Our oceans are a great source of biodiversity, yet there is no single authority which is responsible for looking into the conservation of marine life. So far, the government has ignored this aspect of the environment. As a result, twenty-five species of fish and amphibians have made it to the list of critically endangered species in India. The list was compiled by the International Union for Conservation of Nature. In 2011, the then Environment Minister, Jairam Ramesh conceded that oceans play a vital role in sequestering carbon and as such are a great asset in combating climate change. He even announced a dedicated focus on conserving marine biodiversity through the integrated coastal zone management committee. It is a step in the right direction but much more needs to be done.

India's forest cover has significantly dropped, as was evident from the India State of Forest Report 2011. There is a decrease of 367 sq km in the forest cover in comparison to the assessment in 2009. The north-eastern states account for one-fourth of the country's forests but in the last two years, 549 sq km of forests has been lost. Forests are essential for an economy. They are not just important ecologically but also economically, as they provide wood, fuelwood and livelihood to many. The government is trying to save the forests from depleting further but it will require a lot of effort. We have to start right away to save our green cover.

Conclusion

It is never too late to set the wrongs right. All one needs is dedication and vision. I have been working at the grass-roots for years now and have seen how the right decision can impact people's lives. We all need to get together in order to create a nation that the world can look up to. We have all the resources; we just need to utilize them to their maximum potential. I am confident that in the next decade or so, India can go back to being the power that it once was—some 500 years ago.

శ్రీ

Anurag Singh Thakur

A Member of Parliament from Hamirpur in Himachal Pradesh, Anurag Singh Thakur belongs to the Bharatiya Janata Party (BJP).

Born in 1974, Thakur is a cricketer and has been involved with sports administration at the highest levels, and has always endeavored to democratise resources and improve playing conditions. At twenty-five, Thakur was the youngest President of the Himachal Pradesh State Cricket Association and soon after, he became the youngest National Selector to select the Indian Junior Cricket Teams. Thakur was also President of the State Rifle Association and General Secretary of the Himachal Pradesh Olympic Association and the Hockey Association of Himachal Pradesh; he is also an Executive Member, Indian Olympic Association and is an honorary Joint Secretary of the BCCI.

He has travelled extensively and is a movie and music enthusiast. Extremely active on various social networks, he has been entrusted with generating support and interest in the BJP among the youth, both in India and the diaspora.

INDIA

No, no—not a commando—she's a
student going to her college!

Safe and Secure India

ANURAG SINGH THAKUR

> Most of our telecommunication is in the hands of
> private players. Many of these are funded by foreign investment.
> The implementation of the nationwide networks by the Centre
> and the States means that most of the government data now
> travels on these networks. There can be various other
> security issues besides data protection.

India became an independent nation-state in 1947 through the process of Partition that was both violent and painful, one which left deep scars on the psyche of its people. For the first time, the international borders of this new nation became an artificial dividing line between its people—a physical barrier that existed on paper but not in the hearts and minds of the people on both sides. The birth of Pakistan and subsequently that of Bangladesh in 1971, created a society engulfed by trauma. It once again underscored the contradictions in the two-nation theory. For India, the task of nation-building began immediately after Independence with the integration of the princely States, continuing till the reorganisation of States.

The driving force behind all these acts was the vision of Sardar Vallabhbhai Patel, one of the founding fathers of independent India, for whom national integration and security were of paramount importance. Along with Jawaharlal Nehru, he believed that if India was to secure its rightful place in the comity of nation-states, then it was extremely important that it became strong, united and secure from within and against the outside world.

In retrospect, the direction of India's national security has been shaped largely by the historical baggage that surrounded its birth as a nation-state. Today, more than sixty years after Independence, when we look to address the issue of national security, we must use our historical experiences as a stepping stone to understand and position ourselves in the present.

WHAT CONSTITUTES NATIONAL SECURITY

In a traditional sense, national security should refer to territorial integrity, maintenance of peace and harmony across the borders and securing a peaceful life for the citizens by maintaining law and order internally. But as we now live in a world with a strongly integrated global economy, threat to the engines of economic growth should be taken as a threat to the country's security. In addition, threats to our energy assets; Information Technology and Communications infrastructure; ports, Exclusive Economic Zones (EEZ) and strategic resources such as border roads, rail and airstrips are other security concerns. We need to define national security more comprehensively to include all that is necessary for India to ensure socio-economic and political stability domestically, regionally and at the international level.

It is necessary to understand the challenges that we face today and those that we are likely to come across in the future. It is important to know our challenges, as that would place us in a position to formulate a strategic policy that will guide us for the present and the future. If we look at the scenario today, it leaves little room for comfort. Internally, we are trying to cope with the challenge from the Maoists, which was once described by Prime Minister Manmohan Singh as the biggest security challenge facing the nation. Externally, we live in a troubled neighbourhood. Although there is little probability of an out-and-out war with any of our neighbours, the situation nevertheless remains volatile.

Let's take the case of our immediate neighbour Pakistan, where the chief of the army and clerics enjoy greater influence in the state's domestic as well as foreign affairs than the president of the country. Decades of propaganda by the state-run machinery and the four wars of 1947, 1965, 1971 and 1999 have continued to strain relations between the countries. Even the slightest advances to thaw the ice bilaterally have been met by scepticism and intense scrutiny, thanks to years of acrimony between the two nations.

More recently, the presence and later killing of al-Qaeda chief Osama bin Laden in the garrison town of Abbottabad in Pakistan not only shocked the world but proved what India had suspected for long—that Pakistan was a safe haven for terrorists. This incident pushed US-Pak relations downhill, forcing a rethink about the US level of engagement with Pakistan and drastic cuts in financial aid.

Today, the international community has realised that Pakistan has failed on various parameters; its economy is in a shambles, its polity fractured and its key institutions at loggerheads with each other. As a nation, it has failed its people. It is acknowledged worldwide as the epicentre of terror. As a country that adopted terror as national policy, Pakistan is positioned as a time bomb for the world community but most specifically for India, which will have to bear the brunt of any kind of fallout that may take place.

The situation in Afghanistan is equally critical. A change in the regime—if the control passes into the hands of the Taliban—would hold dangerous portents for this region. The Chinese build-up in Pakistan-occupied Kashmir (PoK) has been a topic of much discussion recently. China's ambition to become a global superpower has to pass through the regional route. The flexing of muscles through border skirmishes, plans to claim territory in Arunachal Pradesh, building of dams on the River Tsangpo (called Brahmaputra in India) as also the incidents in the South China Sea (in 2010 a Chinese fishing vessel deliberately rammed a Japanese coastguard cutter), are all pointers to the Chinese desire to be assertive in the region. On our eastern border, the Myanmar regime has always been hostage to Chinese influence and has often adopted anti-India postures. Even though Bangladesh shares a huge border with India, and a common history, transmigration of its people into India has been a sticking point in our relations. The terror footprint on its soil is a cause of worry, considering its proximity and the porous border. Similarly, Nepal's unguarded borders with India have often been misused by terror outfits for infiltration as well as escape, after committing crimes in India. And this is despite the special relationship India shares with Nepal. Similarly, the situation of Indian Tamils in Sri Lanka has become a thorn in our relationship, despite years of good relations with our neighbour. This has particularly been exacerbated by the defeat of the Liberation Tigers of Tamil Elam (LTTE) in 2009. So far the Indian government's response has been tepid.

Internally, it's the Maoist problem that threatens India's status as a rising world power. With every passing day, the problem seems to only get worse. In the span of hardly a month in 2012, three successive kidnappings shook the security establishment. In Chhattisgarh's Sukma district, the Maoists kidnapped District Collector Alex Paul Menon and before that a ruling Biju Janata

Dal MLA, Jhina Hikaka, from Odisha's Koraput district. This came days after two Italians were abducted from Kandhamal district in Odisha. With kidnappings and killings being reported almost every other day, there doesn't seem to be an end to the problem. Figures released by the home ministry reveal that as many as 606 people were killed in Naxal violence in 2011. Nearly 60 per cent of the deaths in the country were reported from Chhattisgarh and Jharkhand—the two worst-affected states. And in 2011 alone, Maoists attacked 293 economic and other targets. This is indeed worrisome.

Another major worry is the northeast region, which has always posed different challenges to integration with the mainstream. The slack attitude of the government, coupled by a developmental policy that focuses primarily on how to contain violence and not on democratisation or self-sustenance of the region and its people, is proving to be the stumbling block. Furthermore, the lack of will to speed up integration of the region has created a fertile ground for many violent secessionist movements fuelled partly by foreign interests.

India has one of the longest coastal borders. Coastal security needs a complete overhaul as it became evident post the 26/11 Mumbai terror attacks. Equally important is developing a comprehensive policy on maritime security. The attack of the pirates on Indian vessels off the coast of Somalia has heightened this need. Even aerospace violations need to be addressed and security beefed up.

Towards Securing Our Borders

As one can see, India is today besieged by problems internally and externally. The problems are either domestic or regional in nature. But at a deeper level, the undertones are clearly international in character. So that brings us to the question of whether we are taking the right steps to achieve total national security. If not, where are the gaps? And what should be done to bridge these gaps?

India is an economic power today that few in the world can afford to ignore. We have strong trade and economic ties with all the major economies in the world—the US, EU, BRICS (Brazil, Russia, India, China and South Africa) countries, Japan and Australia. We are a very important regional player with the Association of South East Asian Nations (ASEAN) member states. Besides, India plays a pivotal role in the South Asian Association for Regional Co-operation (SAARC) partnership. All these relationships have ensured that India enjoys an understanding that doesn't breach each other's trust. Unfortunately, this kind of a trust has not been earned from our immediate neighbours, particularly Pakistan.

Even though India has conferred the Most Favoured Nation (MFN) status on Pakistan, the same is yet to be reciprocated. India will have to invest in resources on a much larger scale for this relationship to bear any fruit. Of course, trade is only one of the facets of bilateral cooperation. Equally, there is a need to explore other dimensions such as cooperation in areas of energy and water resources. The Iran-Pakistan-India gas pipeline, which has more or less been shelved by the Indian government owing to US pressure and concerns about Pakistan's inability to secure the flow of gas through its territory, would have been a major step in meeting our energy needs. It would have helped decrease our dependency on West Asia, particularly Saudi Arabia, which remains the primary supplier of crude oil and gas. This would have also helped boost Pakistan's foreign exchange reserves and can be seen as a much needed step towards the restoration of mutual trust in the region.

President Barack Obama's recent advice to Pakistan to adopt a more peaceful approach towards India may not go down well with the hawkish establishment there but then that's the ground reality which would be in the best interest of both the countries.

Thus, it goes without saying that by maintaining cordial relations with the SAARC nations, one can largely ensure external security. But at the same time, India has to be fully prepared to fight any kind of aggression from land, air and the sea which may come from the outside. A strong military capable of offence and defence is the *sine qua non* of robust national security. Along with a strong military, our nuclear capability should be the best in the region. India has always believed in the peaceful uses of nuclear energy. For long after Independence, India restrained itself from developing nuclear weapons. But in 1998, soon after the National Democratic Alliance (NDA) government came to power, it detonated five nuclear weapons in the desert of Rajasthan. This action brought about a huge international outcry but the government stood its ground. The action was in consonance with the philosophy that guides the policy on national security. That is, we do what is in the best interest of our country though it may be unpalatable to others.

In addition to the armed forces, a strong police and paramilitary force are essential. They should be capable enough to pre-empt any movement made by the enemy, especially terror modules which have infiltrated the country. Besides, they have to be fully equipped to deal with the problems of insurgency and Maoist terror. Equally important is to protect and guard our important and strategic installations such as nuclear power reactors, hydro power dams and important research stations such as the Indian National Science Academy, Bangalore; Defence Research and Development Organisation (DRDO); Space Application Centres and many others. And for this, our security forces have to be rigorously trained and equipped.

There is an urgent need for police reforms and modernisation. Unless change is brought about in the police force, much of the law and order problem in the country will not be solved. As we know, the law and order situation is not up to the mark and most citizens live in fear. The image of the police in the minds of the average Indian is troubling, to say the least. There are structural and systemic problems that need to be addressed urgently. The public interface with the police should receive more attention from policymakers. What the Indian public is looking for is certainly a more human face of the police. Excesses committed by the forces are sometimes exploited by ideologues to fan the flames of hatred and secessionism. A better-trained police force would certainly steer clear of such pitfalls.

LOOKING INWARDS

In a way, the issue of national security stacks up as layers of interconnected themes, with roles assigned to various stakeholders which converge finally at the doorstep of the political leadership. A strong political leadership is the bedrock of strong national security. If the leadership inspires trust and confidence, then the various players also take the job seriously and the final outcome is good for all. But a faltering leadership, whose authority rests on questionable foundations, is damaging to the system. Unfortunately, in the current scenario, we find the leadership failing to act decisively. The United Progressive Alliance's (UPA) stand on terror presents an image of India as a state which prefers to go soft on terror. Post the Mumbai terror attacks on 26/11, the state has failed to capitalise on the sentiment generated globally, and thus, pressurise Pakistan to hand over the masterminds of the attacks. Since 2008, there have been several terror attacks but there has been no significant headway in nabbing the culprits. The National Investigation Agency (NIA) is a good concept but its implementation has left everybody doubting its efficacy. The National Intelligence Grid (Natgrid), set up in 2011, is expected to start showing results only after eighteen months. The proposed National Counter Terrorism Centre (NCTC), to be created on the lines of the NCTC in the US, has faced stiff opposition from nine states as its implementation would give sweeping powers to the Centre, thus eroding State jurisdiction on these matters. With our systems still not completely in place, it's important for the political parties to put up a united front when the country's security is threatened. It must be understood that national security is like an edifice. Any little crack in the edifice should be dealt with sternly. It would do us good if we learnt from the US and Israel on how to deal with terror.

A more decisive engagement with the Maoists is the need of the hour. The Maoists have succeeded in persuading people in nearly 83 districts across 9 states to take up arms against the nation. Political opinion is divided as to whether the Maoist problem is merely a law and order problem or a failure of the state's development model. Today, it is the most serious threat to our democracy but sadly, the government doesn't seem to have any solution to tackle it. What needs to be done is that they have to be disarmed and brought to the negotiating table. Only then can any genuine development take place in the affected areas.

The problems in Jammu & Kashmir and the Northeast have brought into focus the role of the Army. There are talks of the Army committing excesses and that they should be removed from the affected regions. There has also been a call to scrap the controversial law, Armed Forces Special Powers Act (AFSPA) which gives armed forces in Kashmir and the Northeast sweeping powers to search, arrest or shoot people. In March 2012, the United Nation's Special Rapporteur on extrajudicial, summary or arbitrary executions, Christof Heyns asked the Indian government to repeal the law, as it clearly violates international law. It is true that the Army should be used only as a last resort to deal with law and order problems of civilian nature. It is also true that AFSPA contains powers that may be affecting the fundamental rights of Indian citizens.

But the AFSPA is a special legislation to protect Army personnel from being charged with an offence for actions undertaken in good faith. By withdrawing this protective shield, they would be exposed to a spate of criminal charges which would demoralise the Armed Forces, and thus affect their fight against terrorists and insurgents. Hence, diluting the AFSPA is not in the interest of India's national security, particularly given the situation in the Valley and the Northeast. What needs to be done instead is to strengthen the civil administration so that the Army's role can be subsequently reduced.

The threat of terrorism is now a pan-India phenomenon. There have been attacks in Pune, Hyderabad, Bangalore and other places, besides the attacks in Mumbai and New Delhi. The repeal of the Prevention of Terrorism Act (POTA) came as a shot in the arm of the terror outfits. Today, they operate with impunity on Indian soil. They have left footprints across several countries. The absence of a strong counter-terrorism legal framework encourages more terrorist activities. A strong anti-terror posture acts as a deterrent. The blasts at the Delhi High Court in 2011 demonstrate the audacity of the terror groups to take on the might of the Indian state. The UPA has maintained that there are enough laws to tackle terrorism in this country. But the law has failed to catch up with the innovations adopted by terror outfits. A clear rethink on the weaknesses of the existing legal systems is the crying need of the hour. The pressures of electoral vote-bank politics should not be allowed to weigh on the minds of lawmakers when it comes to dealing with terror. A strong terror law should not be taken as being prejudiced against any one community. Misuse or abuse of a law has to be handled through appropriate safeguards. Throwing the whole statute out of the window on grounds of alleged misuse would be to throw the baby out with the bathwater. Our current national security compulsions leave no room for doubt that we need a much stronger law at the earliest.

What we also need is to stop quantifying the loss in terms of the number of lives lost. Well, it's an undeniable fact that great numbers of lives are lost to terrorism. The data from the US National Counterterrorism Center (NCTC) listed almost 14,000 people as killed by acts of terrorism world over in 2010. In India, in the same year, 1,902 deaths were reported as listed in the South Asia Terrorism database. But more than dry statistics, it is the psychological and economic impact of terror attacks, such as the one on the Delhi High Court, that has to be gauged. What should worry authorities is the impact it will have on the commuter who may stop using local transport, or the delegation of a foreign multinational that cancels its visit to India. It is India's growth potential that attracts terrorism. Perhaps, it is this realisation among terrorists that attacks in rural areas do not pose as much of a threat to the psyche of the business people as the ones in commercial and political centres.

And what we see in the aftermath of such attacks are merely knee-jerk responses which practically lead to no improvement in our ability to prevent them again. The Delhi High Court blasts took place in the same premises as the one four months earlier. It just proved that no real measures had been taken to tighten security. We need a complete revamp of the intelligence infrastructure; it doesn't necessarily mean greater deployment of personnel but better use of existing ones through the latest technology. One way of doing this could be by providing police officers with smartphones. This would allow them to communicate better and use the information—photos, videos, database, GPS—available to them. The Natgrid project needs to be pursued even more seriously as it shall help collect, link and collate a mine of information at the click of a mouse.

A discussion on national security in today's context cannot be complete without elaborating on the need for ensuring cyber security for India's critical Information and Computer Technology

(ICT) infrastructure. Today, many government and most private transactions are done through the Internet. Huge databases are being built that contain sensitive personal information of citizens and the government. If such information is not protected against data theft or misuse, then it would be an unacceptable compromise on the country's security. Today, most of our telecommunication is in the hands of private players. Many of these players are funded by foreign investment made possible through 74 per cent Foreign Direct Investment. Most of the equipment is imported. The implementation of the nationwide networks by the Centre and the States means that most of the government data now travels on these networks. There can be various other security issues besides data protection: the availability of these networks for communication during emergencies which include even natural disasters is just one example. We have to tread cautiously as worldwide cyber-espionage and attacks are on the rise. The Chinese government is known to run a cyber army of sorts which has been reported to have hacked into the websites of government agencies and embassies. Sadly, India hardly has a well-defined set-up to defend itself against such attacks.

CONCLUSION

We have to adopt a comprehensive approach to deal with all existing and perceived threats from land, sea, air and cyberspace. India must have a multi-pronged approach to engage with its neighbours both politically and economically, to enhance the sense of security along its long border and coastline. Besides, our security apparatus needs to be modernised to meet the challenges of modern warfare. Most importantly, we need to realise that security has more to do with the psychological than the physical impact that it has and be prepared to deal with the same. The bottom line for addressing all internal dissension should be that they are within the constitutional and democratic framework of the country. We must not hesitate to usher in strict legal systems to protect our citizens from terrorist acts. In the end, the political class, which is at the helm of affairs, must agree not to politicise issues which are likely to jeopardise the security of the country. India should remain ever-vigilant and prepared to counter any threat, both to its territorial integrity and core national interests.

౭ఎఙ

Hamdullah Sayeed

A Member of Parliament from Lakshwadeep, Hamdullah Sayeed has represented this beautiful Indian Ocean island since 2009.

Born in 1982, this young politician from the Indian National Congress is an advocate by profession. A sports enthusiast, Sayeed was elected to Parliament when he was twenty-six years old, becoming the youngest Member in the 15th Lok Sabha. Representing a constituency which provides a large number of employees to the shipping industry, Sayeed is a Member, National Shipping Board.

He is also a Member of the Standing Committee on Home affairs, Member, Consultative Committee on Health & Family Welfare and Member, Committee on the Welfare of Scheduled Castes & Scheduled Tribes.

Widely travelled, Sayeed has represented the country on numerous occasions, including at the United Nations Climate Change Conference and the Security Council when India became a non-permanent member of the Council.

INDIA

Sir, the drop-out rate is so high here—the only chap left in the school is the teacher!

Lessons for the Future

HAMDULLAH SAYEED

> A new India shall need a new script. And the best way to script
> a new story is by ensuring that India's 1.2 billion population has
> access to education. I visualise education in India to undergo a
> phenomenal qualitative transformation. This re-thinking process
> shall not only relate education to jobs and positions but also
> lead to a larger, inner self-realisation.

'Where the mind is without fear and the head is held high...'
—Rabindranath Tagore

Nobel laureate Rabindranath Tagore had beautifully described his idea of a free India when he wrote this line in *Gitanjali*, a collection of poems. Despite the innumerable invasions and acts of aggression on India down the ages, the country has held its head high. Its glorious past and cultural diversity has few rivals in the world. Its exemplary fight for freedom from the shackles of the British has inspired, and continues to inspire, similar struggles for independence across the world. Our leaders—Mahatma Gandhi, Jawaharlal Nehru,

Sardar Vallabhbhai Patel, Abul Kalam Azad, Indira Gandhi—were visionaries whose views and ideas are still held in high esteem. To be a citizen of such a country is a matter of pride.

The gloriousness was lost for over a century or two when India passed through the worst phase in its life. But, like a phoenix, it has risen once again. After Independence, India followed a socialist model of economy, which helped in getting India back on its feet after years of subjugation. But in 1990, it switched to a more open economy. The wave of liberalisation which followed, helped India regain its lost glory. Today, the world recognises India as an emerging superpower. Foreign investors are ready to come to India, the economy is booming and the government can now concentrate on spending money to uplift the poor and downtrodden. India's outlook is global, but its zeal, local.

Today, India is a confident nation. The world recognises that it has a unique cultural ethos. As Shashi Tharoor has pointed out, if the United States of America is a melting pot, then India can be dubbed a *thali*—a collection of sumptuous dishes in different bowls. They may not mix with each other, but they combine on the palate to produce a satisfying repast.[1] Further, the end of the Cold War led to the rise of a multipolar world and India is no more a pawn on the world stage but a player in a unique way.[2] After the end of the Cold War, India's standing in foreign affairs has had a qualified transformation, and an example is India being a serious player at G20. Today, India's ideals have shifted from idealism to pragmatism, with economics, knowledge and nuclear power to its credit.[3]

---

[1]'India: from Midnight to the Millennium and Beyond', The 125th Anniversary Jubilee Lecture delivered by Dr Shashi Tharoor, St Stephen's College, New Delhi, 12 November 2005.

[2]David Scott, *Handbook of India's International Relations*, New York: Routledge, 2011, p. 3.

[3]C Raja Mohan, *Crossing the Rubicon: The Shaping of India's Foreign Policy*, New York: Palgrave MacMillan, 2004, p. 4.

In such a scenario, a new India shall need a new script. And the best way to script a new story is by ensuring that India's 1.2 billion population has access to education. My ideas about education have been formed during my experience as a first-term Member of Parliament (Lok Sabha). As I was beginning to write, I was struck by what Sherwood Anderson, a nineteenth century American novelist and short story writer, had said about education: 'The whole object of education is to develop the mind. The mind should be a thing that works.'

RE-LEARNING THE THREE RS

In India, like elsewhere, education is an elaborate affair. Beginning with kindergarten to schools to colleges and then universities, it follows the customary path. But much before we adopted the European pattern of education, India already had a rich legacy of teaching. In ancient times, we had the *gurukul* system, which was basically a traditional residential school for the Hindus. Nalanda, Taxila and Ujjain were reputed *gurukul*s where students from all over the world came to pursue higher studies. Similarly, in medieval India, madrasas became common. They imparted knowledge to the masses and were known for their secular nature. Then, the villages had the *pathshalas*, where the village children received basic education. Mahatma Gandhi is believed to have said that the traditional education system was like a beautiful tree which was destroyed during the British rule.

The British are credited with introducing the present system of education, which was based on the recommendations of Lord Macaulay. Schools and colleges were built and Indian students were exposed to a European style of education. Women were also encouraged to get educated. Great social reformers and educators such as Ishwar Chandra Vidyasagar and Sir Syed Ahmed

Khan contributed significantly to the cause of education. After Independence, the responsibility of education went to the states. This continued till 1976, when education came under both Centre and State control.

A major task immediately after Independence was to increase the dismal literacy rate. In 1947, India's literacy rate was a pathetic 12 per cent. More than six decades later, the progress has been painfully slow, now standing at 74 per cent in 2011. India continues to have the largest illiterate population in the world. This is a huge challenge that the government faces. To fight it, the government is trying its best. The Mid Day Meal Scheme has been an early initiative launched to increase enrolments in schools. In 2001, the government launched the Sarva Shiksha Abhiyan which aims to universalise elementary education for children in the age group of 6-14 years. In 2009, the Right of Children to Free and Compulsory Education Act (RTE) became a reality. It was estimated that nearly eight million children within the age group of 6-14 years were out of school. It is now a challenge for the government to educate this staggering number of children. Equally important is to curb the drop-out rate. Rather shockingly, there has been an increase in the drop-out rate at the primary level in one-third of the states and Union Territories. Progressive states like Tamil Nadu and Gujarat have seen an increase in drop-out ratio from 0.1 per cent to 1.2 per cent and 3.9 per cent to 4.3 per cent respectively between 2009-10 and 2010-12. This comes two years after the RTE has been implemented.

The Mid Day Meal Scheme has been a good initiative and should be made mandatory for all government schools. It would solve the problem of illiteracy to a large extent. The gender disparity, too, needs to be corrected. More girls have to be educated and brought at par with the boys. Effective literacy rates were 82.14 per cent for boys and men and 65.46 per cent for women and girls (age 7 and above) in 2012.

Both public and private sectors have an active role in the Indian education system. But it's the government which is still a major player in primary education. As per the Annual Status of Education Report (ASER) 2011, which is brought out by Pratham, an NGO, India has about 13 lakh elementary government schools and 1.82 lakh private schools. Undoubtedly, a huge chasm exists between rural-urban schools. Private players vie with each other to provide quality schools in urban areas, thus neglecting the smaller towns and villages. However, the flipside of the 'good quality', privately-funded schools in cities is the process of admission and high fees. The problems begin from the time a child steps into the school. Admission to most so-called good schools is almost like fighting a battle and is, in many cases, impossible without 'donations'. It's an open secret that donations, which can go up to a few lakhs in some schools, are demanded from hapless parents for getting their child admitted. And for most parents there is no other way as everyone wants his child to receive the best education. What's even worse is that young children, as old as four years, are put through a grilling interview session which determines their qualifying for the school.

The distinction between a prestigious and a non-prestigious school needs to be seriously questioned. All institutions need to be seen as being equally competent; the onus should lie on the individuals to make the best use of it. Increasingly, seeking admission in a school has become a matter of having economic clout and political connection. Parents who have either of the two can easily secure admission for their wards without the tension that others usually have to go through. A foundation of education built upon such a hollow premise needs to be severely criticised. The schools need to usher in transparency and should strictly follow a policy of 'no-influence'. Only then the beginning of a child's learning process can be honest and fair. Even the fee structure should be worked out in consensus with the government, parents and school authorities. An effort should be made so that the school fees are not exorbitant.

Indian education has been mostly secular, showing high levels of tolerance, diversity and respect for all religions and faiths. This must continue and any attempts to communalise education should be vehemently opposed. Even tampering with the syllabi or introducing dubious elements needs to be checked. Any idea cannot be effective unless people develop the instinct from within to follow it. Along with secular education, India continues to have the age-old system of Vedic schools (*pathshalas)* and madrasas. In recent years, the latter has come under a lot of criticism for its communal teachings and there is an effort by the government to bring them within the mainstream. This measure has to be taken much more seriously.

BEYOND MARKS, PLEASE

A major drawback of our education system is that it is marks-oriented. This doesn't bring out a child's natural talents; rather it kills creativity. Neither does it prepare them for life in the real world. Instead, the emphasis should be on skills. Skill-based education should be introduced in schools and should continue till college. In our present system, which is based on the marks in the annual board examination, it is expected that students will go to college and university after school. As a result, the pressure on colleges in cities is immense as students from smaller towns and villages also flock there for a better education. With limited seats and few colleges vis-à-vis the number of applicants, the pursuit of higher education is reduced to a mockery. The solution here lies in opening more colleges in rural India. Also, the preference for medicine and engineering over pure science or humanities needs to be changed. Students have to be made aware of the various career avenues open after a degree in humanities or pure science. I would like to mention the Bollywood film *3 Idiots* (2009), directed by Rajkumar Hirani. It is an apt commentary on the Indian education system where the young are pressurised to pursue a subject which will get them a good salary and a comfortable life. Pursuit of one's interest is generally dissuaded. Moreover, the system still suffers from a colonial hangover and educators believe in a superior-subordinate relationship. Students are still judged and labelled according to the marks they score and the overall aim of education is to end up with a high paying salary and material comforts in life. All this hampers the growth of an individual and hence the realisation of his true potential. Equally important is to understand the real culture and heritage of India. And this shouldn't be done just through Bollywood. Why can't we include puppetry, theatre, visual arts, sculpture and similar art forms to define the contours of education of the vibrant Indian culture? A revamp is certainly the need of the hour.

The purpose of education should not just be limited to getting a job; it should be to strive to achieve a higher goal, just as Gandhi talked of subordinating our lower self to a higher one in *Hind Swaraj*. Similarly, it should be inculcated in the young minds that no matter which field they choose to pursue their career in, they should be able to contribute to society. They should give back to the people the benefits of their education so that lives can be improved. One has to think: will my education give me the patience to beat the competition with endurance and hard work? It is human tendency to expect the best for oneself, but it is equally important to wish well of others. This realisation has to come from within and this is only possible when our education trains us to think in the right manner. It is very much like the idea espoused by the German thinker Immanuel Kant. I visualise education in India to undergo a phenomenal qualitative transformation. This re-thinking process shall not only relate education to jobs and positions but also lead to a larger inner self-realisation.

EMBRACE NEW TEACHING TOOLS

I always had a dream to pursue a postgraduate degree in a western university. Not that I don't value an Indian degree but the rigours of the syllabi, the reputation and the world-class environment attracted me. But the passing away of my father, PM Sayeed, in 2005 put a halt to those dreams as I became involved full-time in politics. Youngsters today needn't sacrifice their dreams anymore. The Foreign Educational Institution (Regulation of Entry and Operation) Bill 2010, which seeks to regulate the entry and operation of foreign institutions, will provide a chance to get the best of global education at our doorstep. Acts like Prohibition of Unfair Practices in Technical, Medical Educational Institutions and Universities Bill, Educational Tribunal Bill and Accreditation Bill shall go a long way in bringing in major challenges in the education scenario.[4] These will also help in reducing 'brain drain' as graduates from premier institutions such as the Indian Institute of Technology and Indian Institute of Management will not migrate to foreign lands for work. This will further help in offering better facilities to work in India and also contribute to research and development.

Unfortunately, teachers are not given due respect anymore. Also, not much effort is made to upgrade their skills and train them to prepare future citizens of the country. Incentives need to be given to attract the best people to the teaching profession. In addition, they have to be regularly rewarded in order to keep their morale high. India is one of the few countries where teacher absenteeism is a serious problem. A study on corruption in education released in 2011 by UNESCO's International Institute of Educational Planning found 25 per cent teacher absenteeism in India, second only to Uganda. If we don't take any measures to stop this, our education

---

[4]'Foreign University Bill gets Cabinet Nod', *The Times of India*, New Delhi, 15 March 2010.

will suffer severely. Also, there is a need to put an end to favouritism in university selections.

Flow of information is *sine qua non* for socio-economic development in sectors like education. With a revolution in the telecom sector and Internet penetration on the increase, the divide between rural and urban India is decreasing. E-learning, distance learning, development of software in regional languages, use of technology as a problem solving device are just some of the benefits of the IT revolution that education will benefit from. Hopefully, this familiarisation with technology will make more people tech-savvy, including politicians who can be connected to their electorate 24X7. A holistic education will result in blossoming of creativity and all-round success. Indian minds shall capture the imagination of all with their innovation, hard work and efficiency.

In a democracy, the differences are often irreconcilable and the idea of a fully rational consensus is too tough a goal to reach. The legitimacy of a democratic institution is reflected when decisions have an impartial standpoint and all stakeholders are involved.[5] The education process should be such that it makes Indians sensitive, tolerant and respectful of differences, varied social and cultural ethos and our distinct capabilities. Only then can we together realise the larger values of democracy, the foundation of which is unity in diversity.

CONCLUSION

Only a nation which is serious about educating its citizens can successfully progress. I am confident that in the next few years India will be able to realise the dream of a literate population. Good quality schools, proper infrastructure, improved student-teacher ratio, less drop-out rates—these and many other problems in our education system will be addressed. It's this vision of India that I firmly believe in.

---

[5]Chantal Mouffe, Deliberative Democracy or Agonistic Pluralism, The Political Science Series, Institute for Advanced Studies, Vienna, December 2000.

Baijayant 'Jay' Panda

A Member of Parliament from the Biju Janata Dal, Baijayant 'Jay' Panda represents the new face of Indian politics.

Born in 1964, he was educated at the Michigan Technical Institute and had alternate corporate careers before choosing to serve the nation through politics in 2009 as a popular representative from Kendrapara, Odisha. Panda was an active participant in forming the Young Parliamentarians Forum (YPF) and is the chairperson of the India USA Forum of Parliamentarians. He was awarded the 'Bharat Asmita National Award' for best parliamentary practices in 2008. He has been a Member of the Parliamentary Committees on Energy, Urban Development and Finance.

Panda has been associated with the Citizens' Alliance Against Malnutrition, an advocacy group which includes many parliamentarians across parties, actors, civil society activists and non-governmental organisations. The Citizens' Alliance has undertaken numerous initiatives to battle child malnutrition in India and engages with media organisations to highlight the issue.

Panda holds a private pilot's license and skydiving and bungee jumping are among his interests.

INDIA

Nobody bothers what's the candidate's name!

Fast-tracking Development

JAY PANDA

> Once we reach a stage where citizens don't think it is
> normal to pay bribes to get work done, that's when we can call
> ourselves developed—not just in the economic sense
> but also in the social sense.

Year 1993: Unthinkable is the dream of India as a potential economic superpower.

Year 2013: The Indian elephant marches on confidently. It is no more foolish to believe that India is on its way to becoming an economic superpower. Years of being labelled as a developing nation will then be over and we will pride ourselves as a developed country. The only caution that we need to follow is not to stop our amazing growth story.

True, poverty will not be eradicated completely but in the next 7-8 years we would clearly have demonstrated that it can be largely defeated—a significant number of Indians would have been pulled out of the poverty trap, and there would be a clear road map for uplifting the others. Along with economic development, there have been concerted efforts to empower backward castes and bring in social reforms. All these measures are steps towards becoming a developed nation.

INDIA VERSUS CHINA

The sluggish growth rate of the Indian economy (3.5 per cent consistently during the 1950s through the 1980s) led to the coining of the term 'Hindu' rate of growth. This term lost its relevance once the economic reforms started in 1991. Thereafter, the rate of growth went up first to 5-5.5 per cent and by the end of the 90s, reached 7 per cent by 2001. In the last decade, we achieved 8 per cent annual growth rate—a major achievement for India. It is noteworthy that the Gross Domestic Product (GDP) in India expanded to 7.7 per cent in the second quarter of 2011 over the previous quarter. From 2000-11, on an average, the country's quarterly GDP grew by 7.45 per cent, and it reached the historical high of 11.8 per cent in December 2003. This is in comparison with the record low of 1.6 per cent in December 2002.

We managed this growth rate post-Liberalisation. Before that, we resisted the opening of the economy and let other South East Asian countries race past us. Thailand, Singapore, Malaysia were some of the countries which realised the benefits of adopting an economic model that would enhance their standards of living. Little wonder then that these countries roared ahead while we were left behind.

It was only when China started achieving a growth rate of 9 per cent and above, that we were shaken out of our stupor. Despite our differences, the fact remains that India and China are identical in some respects. Both the countries have a billion plus population and rather interestingly, their standard of living and economies were similar for decades. In the 60s, the quantity of steel output in India was the same as in China; even the per capita income in India was similar to China. But our systems were different. China had Communist governments while we had a democracy. Things, however, took a different turn when China radically changed its economic policies in the 1970-80s. It shut itself off from the world and there was little information on what was going on in China. After years of isolation, suddenly, China re-emerged on the world's radar in 1990 with its economic reforms and major developments. It made the world—and India—sit up and take notice. Today, it has been recognised as a major economic force, and one of the pillars on which the world's economy stands.

And how does it compare with India? China is far ahead of us. Consider these facts: China's per capita income level is three times that of India, which means that the average Chinese is three times richer than the average Indian. China is a significant military power and exerts its influence on major world events. It's incredible how it has achieved all this in a space of fifteen years.

China's growth story doesn't stop there. As per a Goldman Sachs report in 2010, our neighbour might surpass the US in equity market capitalisation by 2030. It will then be the single largest equity market in the world. In late 2010, for the first time, China surpassed Japan's GDP, with the former's GDP standing at $5.88 trillion compared to the latter's at $5.47 trillion. China, thus, became the world's second-largest economy after the United States.

Ironically, China has a market economy despite a Communist leadership. In India, on the other hand, in the last two decades, our mixed economy was dominated by the government and public sector. Today, things stand differently; there is more of a market presence in the economy. But still, we certainly can't be called a market economy completely. There continue to be many restraints and hurdles in place.

And we need to overcome these and sustain our reforms if we have to catch up with China. That looks tough unless we sustain our political will, which has not always been consistent. We managed to grow only by 6.1 per cent in the fourth quarter of 2012. This was due to the poor performance of the manufacturing sector. Our economic growth went down to 6.2 per cent in 2011-12 from 8.5 per cent in 2010-11 due to decreasing farm output and construction activities.

Still, it is an established fact that no economy can grow without a considerable amount of investment in infrastructure development. Sadly, Indian infrastructure is still primitive. According to estimates by the World Bank, developing countries need to spend about 7 per cent of their GDP on physical infrastructure to facilitate faster development. If we look at development in countries like the US in the eighteenth or late nineteenth century, in Germany between the two World Wars and again look at the US after the Second World War, we will see tremendous economic growth and improvement in the standards of living. The same can be said of China in the last ten to fifteen years. This remarkable improvement is based on the principle that the governments spend 7 per cent of their GDP every year on infrastructure.

The Union Budget of 2010-11 underscored infrastructure development but was low on impact. It had proposed $37 billion for infrastructure upgradation in rural and urban areas. This amounted to over 46 per cent of the total plan allocation for infrastructure development in the country. But more is needed to boost India's long-term potential rate of growth.

These initiatives pale when compared to China that spends about 11 per cent of its GDP on infrastructure development. It is high time that we scale up the infrastructure development to match global standards. We are hugely underspending on our infrastructure.

NEED TO SPEND ON INFRASTRUCTURE

A major impact of good infrastructure is felt on the common man. A good example to cite is that of Kalahandi in Odisha. One of the poorest districts in the country—it is one of the nineteen districts in Odisha which receive funds from the Backward Regions Grant Fund Programme—it has in the past seen severe drought and starvation. But in recent years, it has emerged as a major rice growing belt in the State. Unfortunately, the full potential of the region has not been realised as the infrastructure is not in place, irrigation facilities are very poor and roads are non-existent. So the cost of growing rice and transporting the crop within the district itself is much more than importing it from Punjab which is 1,500 km away. Things have been changing, thanks to a few schemes launched by the government. The National Highways Development Project (NHDP) and the Pradhan Mantri Gram Sadak Yojana (PMGSY) have been doing great work in connecting villages and making markets accessible to them. In Odisha alone, 6,000 km of roads were sanctioned in 2011. In the next few years, this will help in making the local economy self-sufficient.

There is no denying that infrastructure is extremely important for economic growth. The more we develop our infrastructure, more the chances of people coming out of poverty. If we were to compare India's state in 1990 and today, we will find that Indians are definitely better off. We can reach this consensus by applying the international standards of measuring poverty. In 2008, the World Bank issued a poverty rate with the revised figure of $1.25 per day. By using this standard, the World Bank believes that there are 450 million poor people in India. Data released in March 2012 by the Planning Commission showed that poverty had significantly declined between 2005-06 and 2009-10. The new figures are based on a poverty line that averages ₹672.8 per month in rural areas and ₹859.6 per month in urban areas for 2009-10. The UN Millennium Development Goals Report estimates that India's poverty rate will drop to 22 per cent in 2015. The Report also projects that in southern Asia, it's only in India that the poverty rate will fall from 51 per cent in 1990 to about 22 per cent in 2015. In fact, Odisha and Bihar, once considered laggard states, have been outperforming other states in economic growth and reduction of poverty in recent years.

Let's look at the telecom industry. This is one area where we have made great progress. In the last few years, India has become one of the world's most competitive and fastest growing telecom markets. For fifty years before that, there were only about 3 million telephones, but by October 2012, according to TRAI, subscriber base became 935.18 million. Telecom operators add about ten million mobile subscribers each year. This remarkable growth story has been possible due to the government and contribution of private and public sectors. The liberal policies of the government provided easy market access to telecom equipment and a fair regulatory framework helped to bring telecom services at an affordable price.

When people argue about the need for such huge investments in infrastructure, I always ask a question: when was the last time you paid a bribe to get your telephone connection? Less than ten years ago, it was a fairly common practice. No bribe, no phone connection. But today, a large number of Indians—the majority of whom are less than twenty-five years old (600 million people approx)—have grown up in an era in which it is considered abnormal to pay a bribe to get a telephone connection. Such development has a huge social impact on the country—it leads to most Indians thinking of paying bribe as abnormal. Thus, it's not wrong to say that economic development has an impact far beyond the economy as it reaches the common man.

Once we reach a stage where citizens don't think it is normal to pay bribes to get work done, that is when we can call ourselves developed—not just in the economic sense but also in the social sense.

REORIENT THE EDUCATION SYSTEM

It is ironical that in India, in spite of having world class IITs (Indian Institute of Technology) and IIMs (Indian Institute of Management), we have an inverted pyramid—a small number of students who have access to good quality education. Despite growing investment in education, 25 per cent of the population is still illiterate; only 15 per cent of Indian students reach high school and only 7 per cent of these graduate. In such an abysmal scenario, our focus should be much more on primary and secondary education. We must ensure that a sizeable section of society at least reaches this level. The kind of college education we have is obsolete; we need more emphasis on vocational training and professional courses. There is a significant population of graduates in the country who remain jobless or face a tough time finding a good job. However, in the present scenario, being computer literate ensures a job in an outsourcing industry. Similarly, someone with a diploma in nursing has a bright future, considering the lack of trained medical professionals in the country.

We need to reorient our education pattern. Although efforts are being made to devote 6 per cent share of the GDP towards the educational sector, the performance has definitely fallen short of expectations. Expenditure on education has steadily risen from 0.64 per cent of the GDP in 1951-52 to 2.31 per cent in 1970-71 and thereafter, reaching the peak of 4.26 per cent in 2000-01. However, it declined to 3.49 per cent in 2004-05. There is a definite need to step up again. As a proportion of total government expenditure, it has declined from around 11.1 per cent in 2000-01 to around 9.98 per cent during the UPA rule, even though ideally it should be around 20 per cent of the total budget.

A lot of good work is being done in the field of education by various people and organisations. One of the institutions that I hold in high regard is the Azim Premji Foundation, which is focussed on education. Yet, such institutions are just small drops in the large ocean of education. The state of education in India is far from satisfactory. In 2009, the Right to Education Act (RTE) came into force to ensure free and compulsory elementary education to a child till the age of fourteen. In the Budget of 2013, the government has allocated ₹65,867 crore to implement RTE. But it seems this isn't enough to implement the Act. Such low funds result in dismal condition of school infrastructure. The reality is before us: in many villages, there are no proper school buildings, which force the students to study in the open. Many schools don't have toilets. Besides, there is a serious shortage of qualified teachers—India needs over a million of them to fulfil its need.

For things to change, a transparent, honest system has to fall into place. The money which is allocated for improving educational infrastructure should reach the actual beneficiaries. But sadly, that doesn't happen; at least three quarters of the money spent by the government doesn't reach the common man. If we make the Panchayats accountable, then maybe, part of the problem will be solved. Also, we need to connect social responsibility with education. When we educate our youngsters and train them to be medical practitioners, educators, engineers or lawyers, we should inculcate a sense of giving back to society. Only then will we be able to solve the problem of our villages not attracting enough talented professionals. For this, we can always tap into the vast resources available to the private sector.

I have often made a point that now a chunk of the Indian middle class has strong spending power and, therefore, we should not worry about higher education. We can allow the private sector to set up world-class educational institutions. Many institutes are already being set up, but there should be more freedom. The red-tapism and stodgy bureaucracy need to go, in order to bring in more transparency and allow more private players. The government's focus should be on primary and secondary education, leaving higher education to the private sector.

In fact, a public-private partnership can be an answer to many problems in the education sector. For instance, experiments have shown that the private sector is willing to set up schools even in rural areas. Therefore, instead of the government spending money which primarily gets wasted on administration costs, it would be prudent to encourage the private sector.

There is clear evidence, both in rural and urban settings, that in the absence of good quality government schools, parents are forced to send their children to private schools, however shabby they may be. In such a scenario, there is a need to reward schools which deliver results, whether private or public. And one of the ways to do it is to restructure the HRD expenditure on schools. Instead of giving money to schools directly, vouchers can be given to parents so that they can choose which school they wish to send their children to. Later, the schools can reimburse the vouchers.

More Economic Freedom

The right infrastructure and a great education sector are not enough to ensure economic growth. Unless the entrepreneurial energy of Indians is unshackled, it will be tough for India to become a totally developed nation. Studies, facts and figures and anecdotes, clearly establish that even after nearly fifteen years of economic reforms, we are far away from the ideals of a market economy. The US-based Heritage Foundation's 2012 Index of Economic Freedom places India at 123 in a list of 150 countries.

Economic freedom takes into account how much freedom an individual has, to start his own business. Without economic freedom, we cannot move ahead in either infrastructure investment or education. The telecom industry is the only one where we have managed to unleash India's entrepreneurial energies and remove the restraints. As a result, the telecom sector has had huge amounts of economic and social benefits. But for the rest of the sectors to grow, there has to be a greater amount of transparency and openness. The government's resistance to openness goes against democracy. We saw an example of it when efforts were made to amend the Right to Information Bill to make it less transparent. If this attitude doesn't change, then it portends ill for our long-term goal of becoming a developed nation.

POLITICAL DEVELOPMENTS

This brings me to the next thing—how the dynamics of politics will change in the future. I have been in Parliament for the last eleven years and I have raised hackles when I said that caste-based politics will gradually start to fade out. Of course, not many people have appreciated this view, particularly those who have seen clashes, resolutions and parties appealing to vote banks based on caste. The 1990s saw the peak of caste-based politics in India. The whole of north India erupted in violent protests when the former Prime Minister of India, VP Singh, wanted to implement the recommendations of the Mandal Commission Report, which stated that 27 per cent jobs in government services and public sector undertakings be reserved for the backward castes. This was the beginning of widespread caste-based politics as more politicians and parties started appealing for votes on the basis of caste. Many smaller parties won elections on this premise and ended up playing a major role in coalition governments. This has continued till date. But what actually happened after the 1990s was that those parties which were purely based on caste, reached a stage where their vote share stopped rising dramatically. This led to two things: firstly, by the end of the 1990s, the caste-based parties had to widen their base and appeal. Many parties did this by nominating upper caste candidates. And secondly, many parties entered into electoral alliances with the very same parties they had criticised earlier as being an upper caste party. The two major national parties, the BJP and the Congress, have been criticised by many regional parties but they are allies with them now. Caste-based campaigning by political parties plateaued in the 1990s. Caste still remains very significant but is increasingly being overtaken by issues like governance, as was seen by the campaigns and results of various State elections in 2012.

Despite reservations for the backward classes, debates continue on the best ways of empowering the downtrodden. Critics argue that reservations have not shown the desired results and hence, are of no use. But one must remember that reservations are made in order to give equal opportunity and access to education to every citizen of this country. At the same time, it's clear that it is not just religious or backward community empowerment that needs to be addressed. We need to consider the economic parameters too.

I think there is hope in the recent political developments. The 2012 Uttar Pradesh Legislative Assembly elections threw up a surprise. Mayawati's caste-based Bahujan Samaj Party lost the elections, proving that caste wasn't a strong attraction for the voters; rather development and honest governance was. Similarly, the last two elections in Bihar—in 2005 and 2010—proved that after enjoying ten years of empowerment, the backward classes preferred to support development over caste. That is something to be pondered upon. The political class needs to look into this seriously, only then will we be able to move forward.

In the next ten to fifteen years, I believe, caste will lose its appeal though it will continue to play a role in politics. Voters will not be so easily wooed by caste-based politics and political parties will need to make realistic promises to the voters. Development will be the foremost issue and so will be transparency. People are fed up of corruption and lack of basic amenities. According to the popular political mindset, corruption has ceased to matter, but I don't think that's true. In my experience in Odisha, we as a new party—the Biju Janata Dal (BJD)—accepted anti-incumbency as a factor, but got re-elected on the ground that we ran a transparent government, that Chief Minister Naveen Patnaik represented a new, clean system of politics. With that we have achieved credibility and Odisha has certainly turned around. As per the National Sample Survey data, the State economy has grown, in real terms at 2004-05 prices, at an average annual rate of 8.49 per cent in the first four years of the Eleventh Plan despite the global economic slowdown. Bihar has a similar story to tell and, I believe, it's possible for other states to follow suit.

I am hopeful about politics, I know things will change. I don't come from a political family; I come from a business family. Ten years ago, when I would complain about the inequalities, corruption and unfairness around me, my friends would tell me either to stop complaining or do something about it. I felt compelled to get involved. Even if politics and politicians are usually condemned, the fact is that in a democracy, the politicians have the authority vested in them by their office and they shouldn't shirk from it. I believe that politics has acted for good in India in spite of all odds and shortcomings. Compare it to the situation in our neighbouring countries, or other countries across the world, and we will realise how India has stood as a beacon of individual and political freedom and democracy.

Democracies are good in the long run. Many of our problems with our neighbours, I believe, are because they have not consistently been democratic. One of the greatest institutions of our democracy is the Election Commission. Till a decade ago, it was derided by many, but today it is upheld by most. This shows that institutions can overcome reputations. Institution-building can happen only in democracies. And politics can best deliver within a democracy. So I have great hopes for India and its future.

෯෬

Jyotiraditya Scindia

A scion of the Gwalior royal family, Jyotiraditya Scindia represents the Guna constituency of Madhya Pradesh and has been an Indian National Congress Member of Parliament since 2002.

Born in 1971, he has been educated at prestigious institutions like the Doon School, Dehradun, Harvard and Stanford. He worked for a number of corporate houses and was a financial analyst, Morgan Stanley Asia Ltd before finally joining politics. He is Minister of State with Independent Charge of Power. Before this, he held the portfolios of Minister of State for Communication & Information Technology in 2008 and Minister of State for Commerce & Industry from May, 2009 to October, 2012.

A keen golfer and cricketer, swimming, reading and wildlife conservation are his other passions, Jyotiraditya also serves as the President of the Madhya Pradesh Cricket Association.

INDIA

Nice guy—he's built it exclusively
for us from his MPLAD fund!

India's Quest for Inclusive Growth

Jyotiraditya Scindia

> The vision of inclusiveness must go beyond the traditional objective
> of poverty alleviation to encompass equality of opportunity. There
> must be equality of opportunity to all with freedom and dignity,
> and without social or political obstacles.

India stands at an interesting point in its life today. It is a country the world is looking at—in awe, admiration and some amount of puzzlement. The Indian economy is booming, Indians worldwide are being feted and global businesses want a foothold in the burgeoning market. Prime Minister Manmohan Singh rightly said, 'India is an idea whose time has come.'

As the world's largest democratic republic and the home to a substantial English-speaking population, India appears poised to establish itself as a powerful engine for global economic growth. Though India is already the world's fourth-largest economy by purchasing-power parity, the following indicators point to a brighter future: a rising consumer middle class, considerable reduction in poverty levels, competitive business environment, privatisation agenda, thriving services and manufacturing sector. Today, India presents a modern, liberal, open economy to the rest of the world, an economy that is dynamic, thriving and attuned to the forces of globalisation.

Developments in the Indian economy suggest that it is now at a point where it can achieve sustained expansion that can bring a significant improvement in the lives of the people. These positive factors notwithstanding, a major area of focus is to ensure that the growth is such that every Indian—man, woman and child—has an equal opportunity to contribute in changing the destiny of our country.

The twin goals of Indian economic planning have been rapid, all-round economic growth and equitable sharing of the fruits of development. The country has made significant progress in realising the first objective. But the achievements towards the second goal still remain far from satisfactory.

We have come a long way—but we have much more to do. The percentage of the population below the official poverty line has come down. As per the Tendulkar Committee's definition of poverty line, which is close to the World Bank's $1.25 in purchasing power parity, India has reduced the number of poor by 52 million between 2005-10. However, the rate of decline in poverty has not accelerated along with the growth in GDP, and the incidence of poverty among certain marginalised groups, for example the Scheduled Tribes, has a slower decline rate. Indicators of human development such as literacy and education, and maternal and infant mortality rates, show steady improvement, but at the same time, they also suggest that the progress is slow.

These features indicate that while there are significant economic achievements that India can celebrate, it is still far from redeeming the pledge which Jawaharlal Nehru made on the eve of Independence:

The future beckons to us. Whither do we go and what shall be our endeavour? To bring freedom and opportunity to the common man, to the peasants and workers of India; to fight and end poverty and ignorance and disease; to build up a prosperous, democratic and progressive nation, and to create social, economic and political institutions which will ensure justice and fullness of life to every man and woman.

WHY IS 'INCLUSIVENESS' IMPORTANT?

The concern for inclusive growth, or a growth pattern that includes all income strata, is not new. What is different is the urgency to achieve greater inclusiveness—and a nascent realisation that without it, sustained growth will not be possible in the future.

There are different dimensions of inclusive growth. First, there is the crucial connection between income inequality and poverty. Where growth is more inclusive, poverty is reduced more sharply. Globally, a one percentage point growth in income is associated broadly with a decline in poverty by about 2.4 percentage points. If India could raise its response of poverty-reduction to growth to this level, a one percentage point growth could lift roughly 10 million people out of poverty.

Second, the value of inclusive growth in the stability and peace it can promote. Very high levels of disparity can be inimical to democratic functioning, especially when institutions and the rule of law are weak. It is not surprising that the poorest states in the country, where income growth has been relatively weaker, are also the ones with social and economic unrest.

Third, some see greater inclusion as an aid to growth itself. Highly unequal countries see additional constraints to growth compared with more equal ones. As former UN Secretary General Kofi Annan once noted: 'If we cannot make globalisation work for all, in the end it will work for none.'

Finally, without greater inclusion, India will not be able to grow in a sustained way in the coming years. The main reason is that as we come up against increasing resource constraints to growth, it will become increasingly difficult to raise economic growth without a larger share of the population participating in that process.

THE AGRARIAN FOCUS: REDUCE DEPENDENCE AND INCREASE R & D

A significant weakness of the Indian economy is the continued dependence of 52 per cent of the workforce on low-productivity agriculture and allied occupations for employment and living. The efforts made since Independence have led to only a relatively small decline in the percentage of the population dependent on agriculture.

India's area under cultivation has remained constant since the 1970s. Hence, the two ways to improve productivity are: yield management and irrigation. Performance on the yield front has not been satisfactory. Yield growth in all major crops has been negligible. With an increase in population, the yield per person has actually declined. The last time the country saw a productivity boost was during the Green Revolution and the adoption of hybrid crops. With such a huge population dependent on agriculture, India has every reason to push for agricultural research and disseminate such knowledge and practices to farms across the country. If the growth story in India is to be inclusive, farm productivity has to rise for income levels to increase. The research should focus on better farm practices, optimal use of fertilizers and pesticides, productive seed varieties (GM crops), multiple crops on the same land etc. Equally important is the dissemination of such knowledge to farmers.

On the irrigation front, the country should invest in building many more sustainable irrigation projects. These will not only help in easing drought conditions but also provide large-scale employment in the rural areas.

Given India's overall agricultural potential, we have barely touched the tip of the iceberg. It is important to understand that ours is a country where more than half the land is arable, compared to the global average of one tenth. All the fifteen major climates of the world exist in India. There are twenty agro-climatic regions and nearly forty-six out of sixty soil types in the country. Sunshine hours and day lengths are ideally suited for year-round cultivation of crops. India is the centre for biodiversity in plants, animals, insects and micro-organisms. It accounts for 17 per cent animal, 12 per cent plants and 10 per cent fish genetic resources of the globe. A research conducted by Professor N Viswanadham, formerly with National University, Singapore, was published by the Indian School of Business under the Working Paper series. In the paper titled *Can India be the Food Basket for the World?* the author says, 'With 112 million tonnes production, India is the highest producer of milk. India is the fifth largest producer of eggs and sixth largest producer of fish. We produce about 246 million tonnes of foodgrains. India is the second highest fruit and vegetable producer in the world with 134.5 tonnes production but only 10 per cent of the production gets cold storage facility and an estimated 40 per cent goes waste...' The paper suggests a few opportunities for improving the food supply chain. It says that since the food supply chain is temperature-sensitive and manual handling reduces the product quality and life, a third party logistics can be looked into. For instance, there is an urgent need for logistics providers with air-conditioned trucks, automatic handling equipment and trained manpower to provide end-to-end support.

The paper also suggests that certain practices followed by technology-oriented farm sectors in Europe, Australia and North America can be adopted in India. These include data integration, financial flow management, supply-demand matching, collaborative forecasting, information sharing and goods movement synchronisation through efficient transport scheduling. They can result in huge benefits to farmers.

We also have to take lessons from innovative organisations like Brazil's EMBRAPA. The EMBRAPA (Empresa Brasileira de Pesquisa Agropecuária) is the Brazilian Agricultural Research Corporation which is credited for substantial increase in the country's farm production. The total value of Brazil's farm production between 1996–2006 rose from $23 billion to $108 billion or 365 per cent. Brazil increased its beef exports tenfold in a decade, overtaking Australia as the world's largest exporter. It is also the world's largest exporter of poultry, sugarcane and ethanol. Since 1990, its soybean output has risen from 15 million tonnes to over 60 million tonnes. Brazil has done all this without much government subsidy by essentially undertaking a few innovative activities. It poured industrial quantities of lime into the soil to reduce acidity, bred varieties of rhizobium bacteria for nitrogen fixation; brought brachiaria grass from Africa and created crossbred braquiarinha. All these measures helped in producing 20-25 tonnes of grass feed per hectare—many times the native production and three times the yield in Africa; turned soybean into a tropical crop and speeded up the plants' growing period, (cutting 8–12 weeks from the lifecycle), leading to two crops a year; pioneered and encouraged new operational farm techniques like no-till farming and forest-livestock-agriculture integration.

India can learn a lot from Brazil's achievements in agri-farming to bring about a second Green Revolution in the country.

KEY FOCUS: SUSTAINABLE HIGH GROWTH

Growth is not an end in itself. But it makes it possible to achieve other important objectives of individuals and societies. It can save people en masse from poverty and drudgery. It also creates the resources to support healthcare, education and the other Millennium Development Goals (MDG) to which the world has committed itself. In short, growth is a necessary, if not sufficient, condition for broader development.

Some kinds of growth reduce poverty more effectively than others. The distribution of income can change as average incomes rise, becoming more or less equal. The expansion of smallholder farming, for example, cuts poverty quickly, raising the incomes of rural cultivators and reducing the food bill price of the poor. Growth in labour-intensive manufacturing also raises the incomes of the poor.

A growing GDP is evidence of a society getting its collective act together.

As its economy grows, a society becomes more tightly organised, more densely interwoven. A growing economy is one in which energies are better directed; resources better deployed; techniques mastered, then advanced. It is not just about making money. Growth is much more than economics. It also requires committed, credible and capable governments.

DEMOGRAPHIC DIVIDEND AND ITS IMPLICATIONS

India is presently among the world's youngest nations with a median age of 25 years. In Japan the median age is 43 and, in the US 36. Moreover, among the BRICS (Brazil, Russia, India, China and South Africa) nations, India is poised to stay the youngest, with the working age population estimated to rise to 70 per cent by 2030. According to *The World Factbook*, in just over the next five years, as many as 70 million new entrants will be added to India's workforce.

Besides the low cost of labour, the quality of manpower in India is also an important advantage. For example, India annually outputs more than 400,000 engineers, second only to China. Besides the clear demographic and democratic advantage, the drivers for India's growth over the coming decade will continue to be internal consumption.

It is, however, essential to produce a growth process in which employment would be available not only for new entrants to the labour force but also in the non-agricultural sector for workers leaving agriculture. The ability to sustain a labour-intensive growth process depends crucially upon the expansion of skill capabilities in the labour force.

The doors of modern industry will open only to those with good schooling and the relevant skills. For any programme to achieve inclusive growth, education is very important, particularly good quality school education. Apart from opening schools, the working of existing government schools should be improved as a matter of priority. While there are numerous expensive private schools to cater to the needs of the affluent, the poor mostly depend on government schools. Hence, the need is to improve the functioning of government schools without losing more time. There is also a need to expand and modernise teacher-training facilities. In order to attract better talent, it is necessary to improve the emoluments of teachers.

The quality of teaching in our elementary schools leaves much to be desired. Teacher absenteeism is widespread, teachers are not adequately trained and the quality of pedagogy is poor. The massive expansion required in secondary education calls for an expansion in both public schools as well as private aided and unaided schools.

SOCIAL JUSTICE AND EMPOWERMENT

The vision of inclusiveness must go beyond the traditional objective of poverty alleviation to encompass equality of opportunity. There must be equality of opportunity for all, with freedom and dignity, and without social or political obstacles. This can only be ensured by empowerment and participation. Empowerment of disadvantaged and hitherto marginalised groups is, therefore, an essential part of any vision of inclusive growth. India's democratic polity, with the establishment of the third layer of democracy at the Panchayati Raj Institution (PRI) level, provides opportunities for empowerment and participation of all groups in a society. These institutions should be made more effective through greater delegation of power and responsibility at the local level.

Over the years, the governments at the Centre and the States have launched a large number of initiatives at substantial public expense to achieve the objectives of growth with poverty alleviation and inclusiveness. Experience suggests that many of these initiatives have floundered because of poor design, insufficient accountability and also corruption at various levels. Increasingly, there is a demand for effective implementation without which expanded government intervention will be anfructuous. We need to bring about major improvements in governance which would make programmes in critical areas more effective and efficient. The best possible way of achieving this is by involving communities in both the design and implementation of such programmes.

The 73rd and 74th Amendments to the Constitution have led to the establishment of about 250,000 elected institutions of local self-government. As against about 540 directly elected Members of Parliament and about 4,500 directly elected members of our State assemblies, we have about 3.2 million elected representatives in the PRIs. And out of this, as many as 1.2 million are women. There are more elected women in India alone than in the rest of the world put together. It is absolutely critical for the inclusiveness of our growth process that these large numbers of elected representatives in our

PRIs are fully involved in planning, implementing and supervising the delivery of essential public services.

INFRASTRUCTURE FOR INCLUSIVE GROWTH

Good quality infrastructure is the most critical physical requirement for attaining faster growth in a competitive world and also for ensuring investment in backward regions. This includes all-weather roads; round-the-clock availability of power at a stable voltage and frequency; water for irrigation; railways that are not overcrowded, which run on time and do not overcharge for freight; ports with low turnaround time to reduce costs of imports and exports; airports to handle the growing traffic; air services that provide connectivity to all parts of the country; and telecommunications and broadband connectivity to provide the benefits of the Internet to people all over the country.

Broadband connectivity plays an important role not only as a medium but also as a means of bringing knowledge and data through networking to less fortunate institutions. To empower the nation, and to create a world-class ambience for education, science, technology and governance, the country should create a dynamically configurable national multi-gigabit backbone core network. It should be our objective to connect 5,000 institutions of education, science and technology to this core to enable collaborative research and development nationally and internationally. Campuses should be empowered technologically through campus-wide networks and by providing entry devices to the knowledge network in order to derive the full benefits of this effort.

CONCLUSION

Inclusive growth is highest on our development agenda. Our government has launched a very ambitious programme to empower the poor and provide good quality infrastructure to the urban and rural population. Under the flagship scheme called 'Bharat Nirman' (literally meaning Building India), about $40 billion is being spent over a period of five years in the areas of irrigation, rural housing and roads, rural water supply, rural electrification and rural telecommunication connectivity. Similarly, under schemes like the Mahatma Gandhi National Rural Employment Guarantee Act (MGNREGA) and the Jawaharlal Nehru National Urban Renewal Mission (JNNURM), about $8 billion is annually being spent for creating rural and urban infrastructure as well as for enhancing the earning capacity of rural people.

We are a young nation, and an even younger market economy. There is much to be proud of in what we have achieved—sixty-four years of stable and peaceful democracy in this incredibly large and diverse nation; lifting hundreds of millions of people out of poverty; generating vast amounts of resources through successful corporations and entrepreneurs that have competed with companies from the most advanced markets across the globe—all no mean achievements!

It is often said that the twenty-first century is likely to be the 'Asian Century'. I believe that in India we have a more challenging vision and that is to make this century the 'Indian Century'!

৪৩৫২

Kalikesh Singh Deo

Kalikesh Narayan Singh Deo is a Member of Parliament from Bolangir in Odisha and a leader of the Biju Janata Dal.

Born in 1974, he attended the Doon School, Dehradun and graduated in Economics from St Stephen's College, Delhi.

He spent his initial career working in investment banking and with the energy giant, Enron, before being elected to the State Legislative Assembly in 2004. He is currently a Member of the Standing Committee on Petroleum and Natural Gas and was previously Member of Committee on Commerce. He initiated the LAMP (Legislative Assistance to MPs) programme where young graduates assist MPs in legislative research work and is currently its convener. His developmental focus remains primarily on livelihood and climate change issues. He was a speaker at the UN Peace Conference in Bangkok and UN HIV AIDS Conference in Bali. He also led a group of parliamentarians to Nepal to meet the new Leadership and further bilateral relations.

He is an accomplished trap shooter and basketball player, and was also a part of the Indian delegation which went to scale Mt Fuji in Japan.

INDIA

Where's the time to teach, Sir?!
We have to cook, serve, wash dishes...!

Freedom from Hunger and Corruption

Kalikesh Singh Deo

> What the rise of regional parties tells us is that we cannot simply assume a charter of uniform 'national interests' in a country as multifarious as India. Our agendas must arise from the ongoing bottom-up process—one that seeks to progressively negotiate with and give colour to local aspirations.

When looking through the grass-roots microscope, it is not always possible to look into the future and conjure up a favourable image of India, for there always remains so much to be achieved. But when I think of my country ten years from now, I envision it as a developed nation. Development doesn't mean just limiting it to the Gross Domestic Product (GDP) but extending it to social, political and technological spheres, too. In the next decade, India should be in a position to eliminate hunger and poverty completely. It should be able to provide higher levels of social security through accessible and affordable education facilities. I look forward to an education sector which focuses not only on enrolment ratios but on quality teaching and student retention, especially of girls, and strives to reduce the gap between academia and the industry.

Being a Member of Parliament from Kalahandi in Odisha, one of the poorest regions of the country, I am disturbed by hunger and malnutrition. A nation that is unable to fulfil its minimum requisite programme is characterised by its public institution's inability to prevent an ever-enlarging circle of intolerance, violence and disorder, which in turn overwhelms the forces and voices of reason and equity. The Indian state should concentrate on correcting administrative and legal infirmities. Fortunately, some steps have been taken. Various social welfare programmes have been started by the Government of India under the Supreme Court's directive. These include: Annapurna Yojana, Antyodaya Anna Yojana, National Family Benefit Scheme, Integrated Child Development Services, National Maternity Benefit Scheme, Mid Day Meal Scheme, National Pension Scheme and the Targeted Public Distribution Scheme. The order directs the Union and State governments to implement these schemes whole-heartedly as per official guidelines. This, in effect, converts the benefits of these schemes into legal entitlements for the citizens. Further, the court has given directions pertaining to certain other schemes, notably the Sampoorna Gramin Rozgar Yojana. Proper execution of these programmes and policies will go a long way in eliminating malnourishment in Odisha and the country at large.

TACKLING MALNUTRITION

Odisha has a very high incidence of malnutrition. Even while under-nutrition rates have seen a sizeable decrease over the years, the total rates remain high. Increasing cases of severe malnutrition offset the good work done in reducing grade 1 and 2 malnutrition. Despite concerted efforts being made by the Centre as well as the State governments, much work still needs to be done towards addressing this issue. The State government has set itself the target of reducing the rate of malnutrition by a fixed percentage every year. While I am convinced that our approach towards tackling the issue is driven and directed, it must also be said that there are several areas where stricter measures can be taken.

A cursory glance at the data thrown up by the third National Family Health Survey (NFHS), carried out in 2005-06, reveals that significant progress has been made, if one were to simply go by the examined indices. Take, for instance, the fact that malnutrition rates for Odisha among under-three (40 per cent) and under-five (40.7 per cent) children are actually lower than the national average figures (under-three is 40.4 per cent and under-five is 42.5 per cent). While malnutrition in India fell by only 2.3 per cent from 1998-99, Odisha saw a 10 point reduction. There was also a reduction in the Infant Mortality Rate (IMR) from 81 to 64.7 per 1,000 live births that year.

The above facts establish that certain malnutrition reduction interventions have, in fact, worked, notwithstanding the State's sizeable below poverty line (BPL) population. An examination of the secondary data, however, provides more clarity. The decline in rates of malnutrition among moderate and severely malnourished children in the 0-3 year age group in the tribal and Kalahandi-Bolangir-Koraput (KBK) belt has been less rapid than the non-tribal part of the KBK districts, despite a better performance among the former in the implementation of services under the Integrated Child Development Services (ICDS) and other schemes.

A study conducted by the Department of Women and Child Development concluded that reorganising sectoral boundaries, strengthening service delivery through staff placement, regular monitoring at all levels and effective convergence among Health, ICDS, Rural Water Supply and Sanitation (RWSS), would help to increase the impact of the ICDS programme.

If at the end of thirty-five years, a mere fraction of children in this country benefited from the world's largest children's programme ever, it is a sad reflection on the authorities implementing it. The Government of India-sponsored ICDS, launched in 1975, was an extraordinary and ambitious programme that was meant to eradicate the two worst threats to childhood — infant and maternal mortality. In addition, it also envisaged a healthy infancy through wholesome nutrition and proper immunisation against childhood diseases. Education on family welfare completed the picture. But the real picture, as revealed by the third NFHS, shows that almost half of India's children under five (48 per cent) are chronically malnourished and 7 out of 10 young children are anaemic.

A survey carried out by the country's top audit watchdog, the Comptroller and Auditor General of India (CAG), in schools running the Mid Day Meal scheme revealed gross misuse of funds resulting in substandard nutrition and gross irregularities. The report was published in 2009. But such reports have left the authorities unperturbed. Instead of taking remedial measures, the respective governments have only increased the number of Anganwadis.

The fact that the Government of India does not treat severe acute malnutrition (SAM) as a disease is almost a crime. The third NFHS estimates around eight million under-five children suffering from SAM. The normal course of treatment for chronic cases is hospitalisation of the patient. But in most cases, treatment is through feeding Ready-to-use Therapeutic Food (RUTF), a peanut-based paste, high in calories and nutrients, to the children. Several African countries have been using RUTF. But the Indian government continues to delay allowing the use of RUTF as a sustained treatment because it is strongly in favour of hot-cooked meals to treat malnutrition. But more than these measures, a strong political will is required to win our battle against malnutrition.

ROOTING OUT CORRUPTION

It's imperative to remove the deep-rooted administrative and procedural corruption as early as possible. Along with ombudsmen at the Centre and the State levels, the local governments should also be given more powers to deal with corruption. It is idealistic to think of a corruption-free India, but I envision a country in which, at the least, the corrupt are convicted and punished within a reasonable period of time.

Talking of corruption and political will, it should also be mentioned that our political establishment has not been able to keep pace with this age of information. The era of idealistic nation-building of the 1950s and 1960s has been replaced by the era of aspiring and ambitious youth who want only the best for themselves, with little interest in the welfare of the country. The system itself has transformed to reflect and encourage these individuals to chart their own growth.

The change in demographics is not merely limited to age but is also reflected in the increase in education, awareness and urbanisation of India. Large-scale migration to cities is a result of the growing aspirations of the rural youth. The focus has shifted from ensuring two square meals to attempting to lead a life of luxury. The availability of the Internet and widespread reach of mobile phones have ensured that information is available at a click.

This means that political constituencies are evolving to accommodate this fast growing, well connected and easily dissatisfied Indian youth. A large number of parliamentary constituencies have now become urbanised after delimitation. The middle class, considered at one time to be on the fringes of democracy, has now found critical mass due to the massive swell in its numbers and a strong medium of communication via Twitter and Facebook. The evidence of its power was first demonstrated in the success of the 'Pink Chaddi' campaign. This campaign was started by a group of young women in response to violent attacks by the Sri Ram Sene, an orthodox group, on some women in a pub in Mangalore. The 'Pink Chaddi' campaign was a non-violent protest by sending pink underwear to Pramod Muthalik, the Sena's chief, on Valentine's Day. This happened in 2009 and since then, no one has heard of the Sri Ram Sene. However, the majority of the political establishments have failed to take into account the changing needs of its voters. Remnants of Nehru's socialistic rural agenda continue to dominate our political strategy.

CHANGING FACE OF INDIAN POLITICS

Politics has been changing in slow phases. The first was characterised by single party dominance, which was followed by a multi-party system and then the current phase where there is predominance of regional political parties in the country. All through, it has been assumed that popular concerns are being addressed with the changing political scenario in the country. This was, however, challenged when thousands of people took to the streets in 2011 in support of Anna Hazare and the Lokpal movement. Though we have a representative democratic system in place, Indians today are striving for a more participatory democracy. The role of civil society, visual and social media and other voluntary organisations is a manifestation of this fact. The participation of middle class and youth in support of the Lokpal movement shows the changing political scenario in the country.

India's democracy will now have to incorporate this new political class and allow them to participate. Political parties that do not accommodate these rising voices will fade into oblivion. This effectively means that the face of the modern politician is going to change. As long as India believes in democracy, the focus needs to be on reforming rather than undermining its democratic institutions. Politics continues to impact the lives of almost every Indian in some way. For all those who supported Anna and want to be the 'agents of change', politics still continues to be their best platform for realising this dream.

It is here that I question myself as to why this movement instilled a threat perception within the government. This has been a positive transformation that brought corruption to the centrestage. The adversarial tone of Team Anna trying to besiege Parliament contributed to the unproductive environment. Abusive language and name-calling only served to vitiate the atmosphere further. Yet, listening to the voices would have been more politically prudent. After all, Parliament remains the sole harbinger of legislation.

At a time when the credibility of the political class is at its lowest, there is a crying need for introspection. Yet I wonder, in these times, when children of judges practice law in courts and promoters of public companies continue awarding contracts to friends and relatives, why only the conflicts of interest involving politicians are questioned. I attribute it to the inherent faith of the people of India in its democracy and the high standards of accountability they expect from their representatives.

There is no doubt that the political system needs reforms, both within the parties and also on the whole. The question I would like to address is whether the era of coalitions representing regional concerns is better or worse than unitary centralised policy. That regional parties have come to be formidable stakeholders of political power is an undeniable fact. Over the last fifteen years we have witnessed their transition from being minor, peripherally operating entities, to becoming major players in the national political playing field. One has also witnessed a correspondingly noticeable increase in the alacrity with which the mainstream parties engage with the regional players—they seem to be almost anxiously aware of their potency.

What realities does the rise of regional political parties point to? Are they a testimony to a failed exercise in nation-building? Do the people of our country identify more with their local aspirations than larger questions of 'national' concern? Do the localised mandates of these parties serve to de-stabilise governments? Is their elevated status indicative of a dysfunctional federal structure?

A survey by the Centre for the Study of Developing Societies (CSDS) on the 2009 General Elections confirmed a startling fact. As many as 70 per cent of those surveyed considered loyalty to their region more important than loyalty to the country. But rather interestingly, this overwhelming regional sentiment did not dictate the voting behaviour. The percentage of valid votes has been increasing, from 46.63 per cent in 1991 to 52.54 per cent in 2009. Furthermore, states where regional parties did well (Odisha, Jharkhand, West Bengal) were not the ones that showed a particularly high regional affiliation. This is particularly surprising when you consider that the Centre has historically ignored these areas.

The contention that regional parties make for a weak affirmation of national identity is not true. Most regional parties are not driven by ideology. They are not so much products of conflict between the Centre and the State as they are a manifestation of divergent political interests not addressed by national players. Most regional parties with significant strongholds in the national arena today are offshoots of two of the leading national parties—the Congress and the Janata Dal.

In fact, national parties have often inadequately represented local concerns. There is a disconnect between the issues raised by national parties—for instance, Ram Setu vs Indo-US Nuclear Deal, and those of direct concern to voters: health, education, infrastructural civic amenities, poverty and employment. The chief ministers of Bihar and Odisha, Nitish Kumar and Naveen Patnaik respectively, have been successful in addressing these concerns of people in their states and hence, have been voted back to power.

Coalition politics is not a consequence of regional parties coming to power as much as it is a failure of the national parties to represent local interests. Who is to say that all Indians agree upon a single, homogenous charter of 'national interests'? Thus, what was assumed to be a greatly effective federal, centralist structure post-Independence is now sustained by an increasing decentralisation. What the rise of regional parties tells us is that we cannot simply assume a charter of uniform 'national interests' in a country as multifarious as India. Our agendas must arise from the ongoing bottom-up process— one that seeks to progressively negotiate with and give colour to local aspirations.

While one could question the desirability of parties having a local focus, we must not forget that many regional parties take up different points through the course of their functioning over several years, often leading to a 'nationalisation' of their agendas. Regional political stalwarts have time and again expressly stated very 'national' interests in coalitions, diverging from their local identity-specific agendas. Thus, we see a broad alignment of coalitions towards the BJP and the Congress. It is only those parties that face the Congress as their main opponents in their state, which stay away from the big duo.

It is true that governments have become increasingly vulnerable with the growth of regional parties. Heads of regional politics have often had their way with their partners in government, perhaps even unapologetically. This, in many ways, makes national policy attuned to diverse interests, over the whims of singular entities. We have perhaps been quick to forget that national parties in coalition governments have shown themselves to be as much a threat to their stability as any regional party. The Congress itself has been guilty of dethroning governments on many an occasion.

Coalitions are not in themselves a model systemically flawed. Many countries do, in fact, operate through extremely stable multi-party coalition regimes. The Indian context, however, is problematic in the absence of rigidly drawn ideological considerations. This allows parties the luxury of changing their political stance without being punished by their supporters. When policy debates and ideological considerations do not drive electoral politics as much as personalities and caste loyalties, unstable coalitions are then an inevitable consequence.

CONCLUSION

The future portends towards an increase in the strength of regional parties and a corresponding loosening of the Centre's stranglehold. The Centre would, thus, do well to accept the crucial pertinence of articulating 'regional' concerns as part of its broader national mandate. I also hope that both the Centre and the States will work towards a more cooperative federalism.

Not only domestically and regionally, India should advance internationally too—on trade, security, communication and in the cultural fields. India should move closer to its dream of becoming a superpower and playing a more significant role in the United Nations and World Trade Organization and should be leading the developing world at international forums, especially in climate change issues. We need the right kind of leaders who have the commitment, the dedication and the vision to take the country along with them to the next level of growth.

ॐ

MB Rajesh

Working his way up from the grass-roots of the political system, MB Rajesh belongs to the Communist Party of India (Marxist). Rajesh was elected to the Lok Sabha from the Palakkad constituency of Kerala in 2009 and is a Member, Committee on Energy.

Born in 1971, he has been associated with the Student Federation of India, and the Democratic Youth Federation of India.

A dedicated Left-thinker and advocate by profession, he has written extensively on the socio-political problems that plague the country, and is the editor of a Malayalam monthly called *Yuvadhara*. As an activist, he has taken to the streets on numerous occasions to protest against the commercialisation of education, among other things. He has written numerous articles on various subjects in newspapers and periodicals and is an eloquent public speaker.

He is a music aficionado.

They've stopped making such honest leaders
any more! His name has recently figured
in a mere ₹15 crore scam!

Rethinking Reforms

MB Rajesh

> Food security should be given top priority as a national goal.
> Food security can be ensured only when our people can have
> access to food at affordable prices. Poverty and malnutrition
> are not because of non-availability of food in the market,
> but because of the inability to purchase it.

In his emotionally charged momentous midnight address on 14 August 1947, Jawaharlal Nehru shared his dream and vision of freedom with the people of India. He said, 'The service of India means the service of the millions who suffer. It means the ending of poverty and ignorance and disease and inequality of opportunity.' The ambition of the greatest man of our generation had been to wipe every tear from every eye. Again in 1955, moving a resolution on the socialist pattern of society at the Avadi session of the AICC, Nehru stressed the need to provide more purchasing power to people, raising their standard of living and equitable distribution. The country moved on the path of Nehruvian policies for more than four decades until the embracement of neo-liberal economic reforms in 1991.

The man who is the main architect of these reforms, Manmohan Singh, the then finance minister and present prime minister, in his budget speech on 29 February 1992 that marked the break from Nehruvian policies, announced the objectives of reforms in these words: 'This budget represents a contribution to the successful implementation of this great national enterprise of building an India free of war, want and exploitation, India worthy of the dreams of the founding fathers of our republic.' Now the country has completed two decades of the so-called reforms—policies of globalisation, liberalisation and privatisation—and we are going to witness an acceleration of this process in the coming months, with the further opening up of sectors like retail, insurance, banking, civil aviation etc.

It's high time we started thinking about what has happened to the dreams of our founding fathers which we often refer to. Are we anywhere near the much-lauded objectives of ending poverty, ignorance, disease and inequality? Whether we have moved closer to the stated aim of ending exploitation or have we made endless avenues of exploitation? Have we been wiping tears or filling more eyes with unending tears? We really need to have a thorough understanding of the ground realities and only an in-depth introspection will help us arrive at the correct conclusions on the basis of this reality check. And it is through such introspection that we can evolve an alternative vision of building the nation.

Ensuring food for all is the foremost task of any nation. Where do we stand in this regard? The latest Global Hunger Report 2012, released by the World Bank, ranked India 65 among 79 countries assessed. Even Pakistan and Nepal are ranked higher than India. In 2011, India was ranked 67 out of 81 countries; lower in rank to a country like Rwanda ravaged by civil war. While China, Iran and Brazil have halved their Global Hunger Index (GHI) scores over the last decade, India is one of the countries which has made the least improvements in this period. China reduced the number of undernourished by 58 million and Brazil by 73 per cent between 1990 and 2001. The 2012 Report, describing the performance as 'disappointing', points out that India lagged behind in improving GHI scores despite strong economic growth. The Report further says that the number of undernourished people has been on the rise since the '90s until 2006–08. This means that the livelihood of a vast majority of Indian people is on the decline. The Global Hunger Index is estimated on the basis of three indicators—proportion of undernourished people, underweight children and child mortality. On all of these indicators, our performance is far from satisfactory. This fact is evident from the data given by the UNDP India Human Development Report (HDR) and India Country Report 2011 submitted by the Ministry of Statistics and Programme Implementation to the UN on the Millennium Development Goals (MDG). With regard to one of the most important MDG targets, that is halving the proportion of population suffering from hunger, the government concedes that we are either slow or almost off-track. The Human Development Report 2011 released by the Planning Commission of India admits that nearly 310 million of our people live under the officially defined poverty line. Compare this with the fact that at the time of Independence we had a population of nearly 350 million. Since we started measuring poverty in 1973-74, the number of people below the poverty line has come down by a mere 19 million. It is to be noted that even this poverty line is widely criticised as inadequate for measuring the quantum of poverty in our country.

The India Human Development Report shows that the rural poor in our country were better fed two decades ago than they are today. The overall per capita intake of calories and pulses has fallen by 8 per cent between 1983 and 2004-05 in rural areas and by

3.3 per cent in urban areas. The shocking fact is that there is no state in the country where the hunger index is less than 10. Eminent economist Prof Utsa Patnaik has pointed out that during the very period when the GDP growth rate has been spectacular, absolute poverty has increased by 8 per cent. She has calculated this by adopting a food-energy intake norm, that is those unable to access 2100 calories per person per day in urban India and 2200 calories per person per day in rural India. According to this calculation, the percentages of poor in urban India in rounded figures were 57, 65 and 73 and in rural India 59, 70 and 76 in the years 1993-94, 2004-05 and 2009-10 respectively.

Children are the treasure of the country and they represent the future. Unfortunately, 40 per cent of our children under three years of age are underweight, says the India Country Report 2011 on MDG. As per the MDG target, we have to reduce it to 26 per cent in the next two years. The government itself admits that it is certain to miss this target. At the current rate of progress, the government says, at best we will be able to bring it down to 33 per cent, which means still a third of our children under the age of three years will remain malnourished. India is ranked 128 among 129 countries, according to data on underweight children, with only Timor-Leste behind us. Out of 2.1 million children who die every year, nearly 50 per cent die of malnutrition. A study by the Food and Agriculture Organization (FAO) and World Food Programme (WFP) has pointed out that continuing food inflation will lead to decreasing food consumption, which can reduce key nutrient intake by children during the first 1,000 days of life from conception. This can lead to permanent reduction in the learning capacity of children. This shows the disastrous impact of child malnutrition on the future generations of our country. Despite Prime Minister Manmohan Singh describing malnutrition as a national shame, our progress in tackling the challenge is worse than that of sub-Saharan Africa.

Though we are second only to China in terms of GDP growth, our performance with regard to Infant Mortality Rate (IMR) and Maternal Mortality Rate (MMR) is not at all in keeping with our growth story. According to the government's own estimates, the IMR which should be reduced to 27 per thousand births by 2015 will only be reduced to 44 per thousand births. This is to be viewed in the light of the fact that even Bangladesh has overtaken India in the level and rate of reduction of child mortality. Though the MDG target requires reduction of MMR to 109 per one lakh, we are hoping to reach 139 per one lakh. This means that India will fall short of these targets by 17 and 30 points respectively. Universal immunisation target is likely to fall short by 11 points. More than one-third of Indian women of child bearing age are underweight and nearly two-third are anaemic. Just imagine the fate of the country where these anaemic and underweight women will give birth to future generations. So it's not only our present that is at stake, but our future too.

How are we going to shape our future unless we succeed in realising our immense human potential? We have often been portrayed and projected as a future 'Superpower'. How are we going to translate this 'emerging Superpower' image into reality without ensuring health, education and employment to the people of this country, especially the youth? The story is not very encouraging in other spheres as well. The HDR 2011 has ranked India at 134 out of 187 countries in the world. The ranking is done on the basis of the Human Development Index (HDI) which in turn is calculated by taking into account mainly health and education indicators. It is the backwardness in these areas which has led to such a low overall human development ranking.

Unlike many developed countries, India has the benefit of favourable demographic conditions, 51 per cent of our population is below the age of 25 years and, 66 per cent is below the age of 35 years. In order to take the advantage of the demographic dividend, we should invest massively in this young population by providing health, education and employment. Unfortunately, we have not been doing this. As far as health is concerned, our total expenditure as a percentage of the GDP is less than that of Africa. India has contributed approximately one-fourth of the new global cases of tuberculosis in 2009. Annually 30-40 million Indians are pushed below the poverty line due to rising health costs. And India is also a country which has the fourth largest private healthcare system in the world. Though we need to step up public spending in the health sector in a big way, we are spending only 1.2 per cent of the GDP which is far lower than the 5 per cent norm fixed by the World Health Organization. The World Bank Report 2010 has ranked India 187 out of 200 countries in terms of public spending on healthcare.

Though we are heading towards achieving the MDG target of universal primary education, the survival rate is a major cause of concern. Only 15 per cent of the relevant age group has access to higher education. Private institutions account for four-fifths of the enrolment in professional education and overall it is one-third of the total enrolment. This enlarging space for the private sector in the field of education has definitely affected access, quality and social justice. The norm of spending at least 6 per cent of the GDP on education recommended by the Kothari Commission long back in 1968, still remains a distant dream as we are yet to reach the halfway mark.

Another area where our unprecedented post-reform growth failed to deliver is in generating employment. The recent data unveils a bleak future for millions of young people. The reform-led growth was initially a jobless growth which then turned out as a job-loss growth and now the latest trend is towards a job-loss and growth-loss situation. The national sample survey (by the NSSO) data for 2009-10, points to a drastic decline in employment growth in India from an annual rate of around 2.7 per cent during 2000–05 to only 0.8 per cent during 2005–10. The growth rate of employment has been lagging behind the growth rate of population for quite some time. What is most disturbing is that the unemployment rate for the youth in the age group of 15–29 years remains very high. Another worrying factor is the high prevalence of unemployment among the educated, especially those with a graduate degree or higher qualifications.

The policy thrust on privatisation, emphasis on downsizing of the government, withdrawal of the government from various spheres of economic activity, have all led to the shrinkage of the government's role as the main employer in the organised sector. Dwindling organised sector employment in the country is reflected in the fact that out of a total workforce of 460 million, the share of the organised sector in 2010 was only 28.7 million. Employment growth in the organised sector was a mere 1.9 per cent in 2010. This is the result of a highly lopsided growth propelled by the reform process. The lopsided pattern of growth is obvious when the share of agriculture in the GDP has come down to just about 14 per cent but the workforce dependent on agriculture still remains as high as 52 per cent. Services and industrial sectors which have grown faster than agriculture, failed to generate adequate employment to absorb the surplus workforce from agriculture.

Agriculture, on which the bulk of our population still relies for livelihood, is in deep distress. This unprecedented agrarian distress is the backlash of policies of state withdrawal from supporting agriculture through liberalisation, reduction of public investments and subsidies, lack of cheap credit, etc. These policies have resulted in increased price volatility on the one hand and a sharp rise in the cost of cultivation, rendering agriculture economically unviable and pushing farmers into a debt trap on the other. The acute nature of this agrarian crisis is reflected in the alarming growth of suicides by debt-ridden farmers. According to the National Crime Records Bureau (NCRB), between 1995 and 2010 there were a total of 256,913 suicides of Indian farmers. Since 2003, every minute two farmers commit suicide, around 20 attempt to commit suicide and around 60 desert agriculture. This is the heartbreaking picture of large-scale devastation of life in Bharat, as the rural, backward segment of our country is often described in journalistic language. As opposed to this rural, poor and backward Bharat, there is a modern and vibrant India of a microscopic minority of the rich. We have 55 dollar-billionaires whose combined wealth accounts for one-fourth of our Gross National Income (GNI). Though we are one of the lowest ranking in child malnutrition and have dismal position in human development ranking, we are still ranked fourth in the world in terms of the number of dollar-billionaires. According to the latest World Wealth Report, we have 153,000 High Network Individuals (HNWIs) with $10 million or more as investible surplus. They constitute a miniscule 0.01 per cent of our population and they together account for one-third of our Gross National Income. These High Network Individuals have increased their wealth by 50 per cent since 2008. The top 500 listed corporate companies in the country report that for the three years ending March 2012, they held cash reserves of ₹9.3 lakh crore. What does it mean? An extremely small section of our population has reaped the benefits of the much-hyped growth in the era of neo-liberal reforms.

The cornering of the fruits of growth by a small section has widened inequalities as never before in history. According to the National Commission on Enterprises in the Unorganised Sector, headed by Prof Arjun Sengupta, 77 per cent of India's population is living on ₹20 a day or less than that. The OECD Report 2011 has found that inequality in earnings has doubled in India over the last twenty years, precisely the period since the introduction of neo-liberal reforms. The Report says that India is the worst performer in this regard, among emerging economies. *The Times of India*, on 2 August 2012, on the basis of preliminary findings of the 68th round of the NSSO Survey, reported how the benefits of growth have been gained by the upper crust of our society. The report goes on to state that the poorest 10 per cent in villages spend, on an average, fifteen times less than the top 10 per cent in cities. This period has also witnessed a sharp rise in the share of profits and rent in national income at the expense of wage share that has gone down. This is nothing but the growing concentration of wealth and income in a few hands. Sharpening of inequalities is the result of this concentration. When income and wealth is increasingly concentrated in the hands of a few Indians, the masses experience an unprecedented loss of purchasing power. This is a clear indication that the promised trickle-down has not taken place in the period of economic reforms. The growing concentration of income and wealth with the rich few and diminishing purchasing power of the masses is leading to the shrinkage in aggregate demand. With the contraction of aggregate demand in the economy, the growth itself has become unsustainable. This trend is vindicated by the recent lowering of India's growth rate to 4.9 per cent by IMF from its earlier prediction of 6.2 per cent. So, in order to provide more purchasing power in the hands of the masses, the state must make an active intervention. In this era of neo-liberal reforms, the role and scope of the state has been redefined as a facilitator for private capital. The state must break the limitations of this role and play a proactive role through stepping up public investments in agriculture, social sectors and employment generation.

Do we have any dearth of resources to do so? Not at all. Here are some staggering figures. According to an estimate of the Global

Financial Integrity Report, illegal funds stashed away in foreign banks are worth more than $400 billion, that is more than ₹20 lakh crore! The estimated loss due to some major scams in recent times will be around ₹7 lakh crore. The fountainhead of this gigantic corruption is these very policies. In the neo-liberal era, corruption has become the worst form of primitive capital accumulation. The opening up of our valuable natural resources have created avenues for mega corruption. These huge losses to the exchequer of the country could have been utilised for the much-needed public investments in health, education and employment. India spends less than 5 per cent of its GDP on social protection schemes compared to 15 per cent spent by Brazil, another emerging economy. We could have had more resources at our disposal had we properly tapped our tax potential. According to the Union Budget 2012-13, the total amount of revenue foregone during 2011-12 is ₹81,214.3 crore. As pointed out by eminent journalist P Sainath, the total amount of tax concessions, mainly to the rich, in the last seven years is a mammoth ₹25.7 lakh crore. Can anybody still complain that we don't have enough resources? Hence, it is not a question of lack of resources. It is a question of political will to tap these immense resources, to make use of it for the service of the millions who suffer.

How can these millions be taken out of poverty and suffering? How to improve their plight and build a nation free of hunger, illiteracy and unemployment?

In order to make India a more just and empowered nation, a set of new policies have to be implemented, the first and foremost being comprehensive land reforms. In the period after Independence, we have only seen some token efforts and half-hearted measures for land reforms except in states like Kerala, West Bengal and Tripura. Land reform is the key to breaking the existing concentration of wealth and assets in rural India. Through a re-distribution of wealth and assets, land reforms will generate income, increase demand for goods and services, widen the domestic market and will create employment and more income. Unfortunately, the neo-liberal growth model is characterised by land grab, growing concentration of land ownership, large scale displacement and increasing landlessness. This trend needs to be reversed and land reforms have to be implemented without any further delay.

Secondly, to liberate India from hunger and malnutrition, food security should be given top priority as a national goal. Food security can be ensured only when our people can have access to food at affordable prices. Poverty and malnutrition are not because of non-availability of food in the market, but because of the inability to purchase it. The market cannot ensure access to food at affordable prices. This can only be ensured through a universal public distribution system. The system of targeting should be done away with. Improving and modernising our agriculture is also important to enhance our food production. This has to be done through increased public investment in agriculture with special emphasis on agriculture research and development.

Thirdly, India will have a future only if we succeed in empowering our young people through education and employment. The long-pending dream of earmarking at least 6 per cent of the GDP for education should be fulfilled. In the present scenario, where knowledge in itself has become the capital; generation, dissemination and democratisation of knowledge will be a key factor in development. Access to higher education is an important precondition for the transformation of India into a developed nation.

Speculative capital and the growth led by its profit cannot generate employment. Rapid industrialisation is the way forward for generating the much-needed employment opportunities in the country. Widening of our domestic market, more income and purchasing power are the inevitable prerequisites for rapid industrialisation. However, this industrialisation and development should not be at the cost of the environment. Mindless exploitation of natural resources and greed for profit should not be allowed to go unabated. If we respect our future generations' right to live in this country, we must develop a perspective based on a proper balance between growth and environment.

Regarding our economy, we have to be cautious about the flow of speculative capital, especially at a time when the global economy is experiencing increased volatility. In the interest of the country, the flow of speculative capital (FII) needs to be regulated and Foreign Direct Investment (FDI) has to be made conditional. Foreign Direct Investment should be allowed subject to the goals of enhancing the level of production in the economy, bringing innovative technology and generating employment. The flow of FDI which is in contrast to these goals and is not in the interest of our economy should be discouraged.

Finally, fighting corruption to end the loot of our resources is a challenge that has acquired great importance today. This requires fundamental changes at the political and policy level, putting in place effective legal and administrative mechanisms. All these are issues to be addressed through more active political mobilisation and involvement of the masses.

Unless a strong political will is displayed, the widening divide between the vibrant India of the few super rich and the suffering Bharat of the vast majority of the poor can never be bridged. It has already led to a peculiar situation of a nation within the nation. The time has come to acknowledge this reality and to act immediately. To act doesn't mean more doses of reforms but a serious re-thinking and reversal of the neo-liberal growth trajectory.

೧೦೧

Milind Deora

A Member of Parliament from the Indian National Congress, for the South Mumbai constituency, Milind Deora entered the Lok Sabha in 2004.

Born in 1976, Deora is part of the rising brigade of young politicians who have become the reflection of the change that the youth wish to see in the political, social and economic system of India. Deora is an alumnus of the Sydenham College, Mumbai and Boston University. Deora is involved with underprivileged youth and his NGO named Sparsh, assists fund-starved schools, provides free computer education in over 100 schools, scholarships, and distributes uniforms and textbooks to needy children.

He has held various Committee positions in the Ministry of Defence, Civil Aviation, Estimates, Urban Development and Information Technology. At the time of writing for this book, Deora is the Minister of State for Communications and Information Technology and also holds additional charge as the Minister of State for Shipping. His love for music, especially the Blues, is well known and as an accomplished guitarist he has several performances to his credit. His other hobbies include playing squash and swimming.

INDIA

He's an independent MP—irrespective of who forms the government, he'll be a cabinet minister!

On the Road to Urban Development

MILIND DEORA

> The popular saying 'real India lives in villages' will soon
> lose its meaning. For, in a couple of decades, most of India will be
> living in urban areas, thus making urban development one of
> the greatest challenges of our times.

The twenty-first century has seen India emerge on the global scene as a major player. It has become one of the fastest growing economies in the world today. Though not a developed nation in its true sense, it has done reasonably well in certain areas such as economics and politics. But, there are many more aspects where India is lagging and is faced with tough challenges. It is in overcoming these challenges and addressing its lacunae that India's true success rests.

EMERGING GLOBAL POWER

Globally, India and China are the biggest growth engines. India still outperforms China in various areas despite the fact that China's growth rate (witnessed double-digit growth during 1990-2004) is higher. But India's growth rate is much more equitable and inclusive, and this is because it is more democratic, transparent and open. These parameters will allow India to sustain itself in the next few decades. The economic challenge for India, however, will be to focus on how and where to improve. For instance, one can consider boosting the labour-intensive manufacturing sector, which is among the top ten in the world as per the United Nations Industrial Development Organization Report 2010. The sector accounts for nearly 14 per cent of jobs and should be considered to absorb the ever-growing workforce. Roughly 10 million people are added to India's workforce annually and it is a challenge to absorb them gainfully in one of the sectors. The services sector, which grew by 7.4 per cent in the year 2011-12 and employs nearly 34 per cent, can be the other option for employment. However, this sector is limited to more white-collar jobs and doesn't employ in the same range as manufacturing. On the other hand, agriculture, which employs about 52 per cent of India's workforce, is a viable option for employment. Even though its economic contribution to the GDP may be declining, it continues to play a significant role in the country's socio-economic fabric. Interestingly, sub-sectors such as food processing as well as measures to empower the farmers are helping to strengthen this sector.

The other major challenge that India faces is development among the economically weaker sections of society. The benefits of liberalisation, which started fifteen years ago, have only now started to reach out to society. The Government of India should not abandon this process; it should continue with the liberalisation process because the reforms would have a long-term impact. In India, both short-and long-term reforms are essential, because for any long-term benefit, a short-term fallout is inevitable and would need to be cushioned.

For instance, the government's Mahatma Gandhi National Rural Employment Guarantee Act (MGNREGA) is an effort to provide a temporary social security cushion to those who might be affected by liberalisation. If we open up the economy without installing short-term safety measures, there will be many disgruntled elements which might emerge and damage the process. So, a combination of both short- and long-term reforms is the ideal way to go ahead.

POLITICS IN DEMOCRACY

Let's look at the nature of our governing systems. After the growth of regional parties, we now have a coalition government at the Centre. Coalitions are here to stay. While some consider coalitions as a good indicator of democracy functioning at its best, others see it as a big challenge for India to separate itself from the conflicts of national and regional interests.

But essentially, India is a mixed bag of many dimensions—urban-rural; rich-poor; Hindu-Muslims; backward and forward castes. So, problems have to be tackled at different levels. Usually, political problems are nothing but manifestations of regional aspirations which don't always get noticed by large national parties. In such a scenario, the rise of regional parties, with their focus on regional issues and problems, usually overlooked by the national parties, is only natural. But there can be a danger when these regional parties fuel caste and regional divides.

In a coalition system, there is a definite challenge for India to bring together the aspirations of both national and regional parties and to find some common ground to harmonise their interests. It is hardly surprising that one of the first things that a coalition government tries to do is to draft a common minimum programme which defines the aims and objectives of the coalition. As long as regional parties and governments understand the importance of addressing local aspirations within the context of national welfare and economic development, there is no threat to the democratic fabric of the country.

A serious political challenge that we face is from the neighbouring countries in the form of problems such as insurgency, terrorism, bioterrorism and nuclear threats. As one of the strongest economic nations in Asia, India should deal with these issues economically. Socially, Indian society remains stratified by differences in religion and caste. It is difficult to rid society of these evils easily because political parties bank on these divides to get votes. The only solution is to be vigilant of parties that stratify societies for electoral gain.

One of India's greatest political strengths is the ability to handle bilateral relations with all countries of the world with amazing flexibility. For instance, India can have agreements with the US and Iran, even though the two countries are at loggerheads with each other. Most countries are unable to maintain this kind of political equilibrium. India, however, has accomplished this to a great extent.

While I dream of a developed India a decade from now, I know the road to achieving that status is not going to be smooth. Unless the social parameters are met, a country cannot be fully developed. Mere economic might doesn't really make a country a superpower. India still has a long way to go when it comes to these social parameters like health, education, status of women and children, so on and so forth.

More than the economic and social issues, it's the politics of the country that one needs to worry about. Most political parties agree on the economic agenda for the country but it is the social one that is an area of extreme sensitivity. Each party tries to exploit its political base and represent the interests of respective constituencies. This is natural in a democracy. But at the same time, it is equally important to work towards uplifting and empowering backward communities. As early as possible, we should strive for a fair and egalitarian society where there is no need for reservations. People should be given a chance to stand on their feet and prove their worth on their own merit. That's the only way we can liberate marginalised sections and give them a chance to be part of nation-building.

URBAN DEVELOPMENT: PROBLEMS AND PROGRESS

The popular saying 'real India lives in villages' will soon lose its meaning. For, in a couple of decades, most of India will be living in urban areas, thus making urban development one of the greatest challenges of our times. Twenty-five years ago, around 12 per cent of Indians lived in cities; today that number has increased to 30 per cent. In 1900, 15 per cent of the world population lived in cities; 100 years later this figure went up three times. It is incredible that India took only 25 years to reach urbanisation while the world did it in 100 long years. In a couple of decades from now, the urban population of the world is poised to be about 50 per cent of India's total population. India's urbanisation rate is approximately four times higher than the global average. Therefore, it is a big challenge before us to address the problems of urbanisation.

In some ways, urbanisation is easier and in other ways, more complicated than rural development. It is easier because it does not require managing rivers or land reforms or connecting farmers. It just involves providing basic amenities and infrastructure. But it also has a complex side—unlike a village where usually a homogenous society exists, a city has people from different religions, castes and regions living together. And to have them live harmoniously and peacefully can be a challenge.

First, let us try to understand the economic composition of this 30 per cent of typical urban area. It primarily includes the service sector which accounts for about 57 per cent of the GDP. The manufacturing sector, largely based in urban areas, accounts for almost 14 per cent of the GDP. So, more than 70 per cent of our GDP comes from urban areas where 30 per cent of the population resides.

The urban productivity output is double of what it is in rural areas. In that context, urbanisation can be good as it means higher productivity. If cities and towns are better planned with world-class amenities, they can add to the productivity of a nation. Urbanisation is happening so rapidly that it has caught everyone off-guard. All of a sudden, we are caught in this tussle of demolish-don't demolish, traffic chaos, crumbling public transportation systems, water and electricity shortage, sewage problems, poor sanitation...the list is endless. All the basic amenities are under tremendous strain. In a way, the rapid growth of urbanisation is a good wake-up call for the rest of the nation. Soon this rapid pace of urbanisation will also take smaller towns into its fold and the lessons learnt from the metros can help us be better prepared. At the same time, it is not complicated rocket science that we need to worry about. All that we need is a blueprint and impose it strictly at a national level and involve all states to be a part of the vision. Once we can accomplish this, there will be efficient and standard solutions to the problems arising out of urbanisation.

The classic problem troubling India is that of rapid development with minimal infrastructure planning. It is almost like the problem in the aviation sector where there are a hundred airlines but just a few airports to provide adequate facilities. The practical solution would have been to build airports first and then allow the airlines to operate. However, the traditional approach is safer and better because we should let development happen, allow the market forces to be dominant and eventually, infrastructure will develop. Having said that, in urban areas one can still plan ahead, plan open spaces, areas for public utilities like schools, hospitals and allot areas for the public transportation systems. The Jawaharlal Nehru National Urban Renewal Mission (JNNURM), started by the UPA government in 2006, aims at not just financing the State governments or in giving them money for cities but also creating a blueprint on how to plan out our cities.

FUTURE OF URBANISATION

The future of urbanisation is to build large cities around metros— satellite towns that decongest them. That is the way it is done all over the world. For instance, Manhattan in the US was terribly congested way back in the nineteenth century. The Brooklyn Bridge was built in 1883 with the aim of decongesting Manhattan and spreading that congestion to Queens and Brooklyn. This plan worked very well, and the model continues to work even after a century-and-a-half since its conception. That is the way we need to plan, we need to foresee what's going to happen fifteen years from now in our cities, how are they going to grow and the way they need to be planned. We need to be careful while planning the satellite towns, as their primary purpose is to supplement the main metro rather than become a parallel economic centre. The planning can be done best under a public-private partnership. But the government has to set stringent rules in order to carry forward such a partnership.

Primarily, the government has to create a blueprint. There are many ways the government can issue definite directions to a builder about where he has to really mark out a space for affordable houses within the whole plan of the township, and not simply allow him to build in a way that hampers the growth of the township. The government need not subsidise the land. The market forces can prevail within the ambit of the master plan.

Then, one has to consider the industries. Manufacturing is a large employer and requires cheap land. So, automatically, the manufacturing sector will shift to the outskirts and the satellite towns. The services sector may stay in the metros but with the help of an efficient transportation system, people can live in the satellite towns and work in the metros. To take another example of the US, people live in New Jersey and commute to New York every day for work. The commute takes them just about an hour and this is possible because of an extremely efficient transportation system.

We need to understand that urbanisation is a reality, it is happening around us. It is a natural migration. This movement of people is more for jobs than a better life. There is no point in trying to prevent this migration. The way to urbanisation is to allow people to migrate and to build more cities for them. This will eventually lead to a fall in contribution of agriculture to the country's GDP. Today, this kind of urbanisation is normal all over the world. In India, it is happening very fast. So, to cope with this, we need to create the requisite infrastructure that allows cities to sustain and absorb the increasing number of migrants by providing them:

- Job opportunities
- Affordable housing facilities
- Basic utilities like transportation

DEVOLUTION OF POWER

In any city today, there are multiple agencies implementing things, and these agencies are either under corporations, or under the State government. Huge conflicts arise because they have to work together, but in reality, there is very little coordination. For smoother operations, it is important to devolve powers, invest municipalities with a lot more freedom and power. Most municipalities in our cities are already burdened with the forever-increasing demand in providing better civic amenities, proper sanitation, good schools, inexpensive hospitals, smooth transportation and various other facilities.

URBAN GOVERNANCE

Under this system, authority is given to those who are elected by the people. This is done to ensure better coordination between agencies and in the process allow smooth planning. This should be done as it is better for the future of urban development in India. If we also make one or two nodal agencies, that would help. In large metros and growing cities, the problem of housing and public transportation is severe. Our state governments have to realise that as the economic activity escalates, they must plan ahead. It is essential to integrate progressive thinking into city planning. Planning should not be done in an incremental manner; we should not build excess capacity and allow demand to dictate supply.

When the British planned cities like Mumbai in Maharashtra, they planned for civic, social infrastructure, parks, etc. Thus, it served and lasted the needs of the people. What we now need to do is in similar instances, draft master plans again but not allow construction to come up just anywhere. In cities that already have parks, we do not need parks. Likewise, we need to involve a lot of efficient people to visualise the master plan of a city. We need to see how one city connects to the other, how one economic opportunity connects to another. We need to integrate. This is the kind of planning that State governments should be involved in. At present, people are not involved in the process of urban governance. Corporations are not able to work effectively as they have no executive powers.

Town planning should be in the hands of its people who are elected by the local people. In Delhi, for instance, it would be a challenge to see how this can be implemented because the Delhi Development Authority is not under the State government.

Implementation does not take long. It is the phase between conceiving a plan and finally implementing it that takes long. The government has to realise that it cannot work in all aspects of urban governance. Its expertise may lie in some but not all spheres. So it makes sense to allow private companies. Entry of private companies will ensure speed and show competitive incentive. Within a short period, governments will have to address developing infrastructure such as ports, aviation etc. All of this can be done once we bring governance to the local level and involve locals to help in the development process. Though there are Residential Welfare Associations in many areas, there is still a need for more clarity and consistency in their functioning.

All political parties have to keep aside their politics and look beyond it to see the bigger picture. After all, major cities all over the world had problems of decay and development, but they planned and made things happen. India is doing the same. Our vision is beginning to take form and we are well on the right path.

There is no reason why we can't realise our dream of being a developed nation. The year 2020 is not too far away; if we focus and work towards our goal with dedication, the world can look up to India as a superpower.

ℰᏂᏌᎡᏁ

Nishikant Dubey

Nishikant Dubey is a Member of Parliament from Godda constituency of Jharkhand, and a leader of the Bharatiya Janata Party. Born in 1969, Dubey has a degree in business administration from the prestigious Faculty of Management Studies at Delhi University. He was a businessperson and agriculturist before he joined active politics.

Dubey started as a youngster in the student wing of the BJP, the Akhil Bharatiya Vidyarthi Parishad, and the Swadeshi Jagran Manch. His success in the Lok Sabha elections can be attributed to the support of a large number of young voters, for whom he is keen to create an inclusive, egalitarian society.

A sports enthusiast and music lover, he is involved with various charitable and educational trusts. He turns to spiritual discourses for comfort, and has travelled widely in his political career.

INDIA

So what if you're a veterinary doctor?!
At most of the hospitals they treat us like animals!

Bridging the
Urban-Rural Divide

NISHIKANT DUBEY

> By building the right infrastructure, providing quality healthcare to
> all and tackling threats to the country's security, the government can
> bring the two Indias closer. Let there be only one Bharat,
> the one the whole world will look up to.

India's economic growth story is the one that inspires and amazes. For years after Independence, the nation was a socialist state, characterised by extensive regulations, protection and public ownership. This majorly resulted in widespread corruption and slow growth. Those were the days when foreign investors shied away from even looking at India. But in 1991, a historic change took place when the country moved towards a market-based economy. The economic liberalisation initiated a series of changes which eventually established India in 2008 as one of the fastest growing economies in the world.

The benefits of economic growth were largely enjoyed by a burgeoning middle class and the wealthy lot. Unfortunately, and rather adversely, rural India got left behind in this economic boom. Agriculture, which is a source of livelihood for the majority of rural India, managed a pathetic 2 per cent growth vis-à-vis manufacturing and service industries. The divide has only become worse over the years, with little effort from the government to effectively bridge it. If India has to grow and become a superpower, it has to concentrate on inclusive growth. And for that, the great divide has to be bridged.

GLARING DISCONNECT

The gap between the two Indias—urban and rural—has always been there. After Independence, as India set out to rebuild its economy and launched the Five Year Plans, the emphasis was largely on developing the urban areas. The focus on villages was not prominent. Yet, it didn't show because the difference wasn't so glaring. But after the economic boom, the differences are impossible to ignore. In some parts, the development has been lopsided and in some others, it has been completely ignored. If we take the example of the eastern part of India, it becomes clear how this area has been subject to sheer negligence, leading to a yawning gap.

The eastern belt of India—Jharkhand, Odisha, West Bengal— has one of the richest mineral deposits in the country. It has been called the 'mineral heartland of India', what with 93 per cent iron ore, 84 per cent coal, 100 per cent kyanite, 70 per cent chromite, 70 per cent mica, 50 per cent fire clay, 45 per cent asbestos, 20 per cent limestone, 10 per cent manganese and 45 per cent china clay to be found there. Since Independence, the country's demand for coal, iron ore and other minerals has been met primarily by this region. In such a scenario, this region should have been the richest and most prosperous in the country.

The reality, however, is the opposite. Ironically, these states are today the most backward regions in the country. A telling example is my constituency, Godda, in Jharkhand. It has Asia's largest coal block, the Lalmatia Colliery. Yet, in 2006, the Government of India had to declare Godda as one of the country's most backward districts. It continues to receive funds from the Backward Regions Grant Fund Programme (BRGFP). Nearly 70 per cent of people in the region are Below Poverty Line (BPL); 70-75 per cent women are anaemic and 60 per cent of children are malnourished. There is no medical college or hospital, the lone district hospital lacks basic facilities like oxygen. The state of education is pathetic—government schools have no teachers. Basic infrastructure such as roads is missing. Godda gets electricity for only 2-3 hours in a day. Most irrigation projects are shut. Despite having the largest coal block, no power plant has been built in this region. And this, by and large, is the story of the rest of rural Jharkhand, which supplies the requisite minerals to fuel the country's economy. But the monetary returns don't come to Jharkhand; rather they go to the metros. A good example is the Tata story. They built the steel plant in Jamshedpur in 1906. They developed the area, built hospitals, schools, colleges and the basic infrastructure. But all these were meant for the people working in their steel plants. Nothing was meant for the locals who gave up their land. All the profits that they made from producing steel, went to building a state-of-the-art hospital in Mumbai or a science centre in Bangalore. They dug the earth for profits but didn't share any of it with the locals. Similarly, all the coal from Godda goes to the Farakka Super Thermal Power Station in West Bengal and Punjab, which benefit from its use. In another instance, the Massanjore Dam on the Mayurakshi river, which originates near Deoghar in Jharkhand, is benefitting West Bengal. Both irrigation and drinking water facilities are enjoyed by the State. The Damodar Valley Corporation, India's first multipurpose river valley project generating thermal and hydro-power, has a network of four dams. But they are all controlled by West Bengal. Such examples are countless. This disparity is too glaring. It is time we realised that states like Jharkhand may be poor economically, but in reality they are the richest. What has made them poor is the indiscriminate plundering of their wealth, without any profits coming their way.

The Government of India launched the Bharat Nirman programme in 2005 for creating basic rural infrastructure. It included, among other things, providing safe drinking water and electricity to all rural households, connecting villages with all-weather roads and bringing one crore hectare land under irrigation. Indeed a laudable scheme, but it has not achieved its full potential. It is one scheme that can actually bridge this great divide. If the basic infrastructure is provided in the villages and smaller towns, then there will be more opportunities for them to grow and develop. Thus, the need is to provide the basic infrastructure so that growth comes to the remotest parts of the country.

It is indeed sad that the government has launched so many schemes but few of them have been successful and many don't even make sense. The Rajiv Gandhi Grameen Vidyutikaran Yojana (RGGVY) is a clear example of a sheer waste of money. It aims to provide electricity to Below Poverty Line (BPL) households in the villages, leaving out those who are Above Poverty Line (APL). How can it be assumed that APL families don't need electricity or can easily buy it? Such a scheme only leaves the villagers divided and don't really benefit anyone.

Instead of launching too many schemes, some of which may overlap, the aim should be to have a few but focussed programmes. It makes coordination between different agencies easier. And that in turn will give way to quick implementation of projects. Also, it reduces corruption.

In my constituency, I am trying to bring about some changes. For the first time in sixty-five years, 127 kilometres of railway tracks have been laid out in Godda. That will really boost its development. Also, four new engineering colleges, a medical college hospital, eight new Industrial Training Institutes (ITIs) and three polytechnics will provide an array of career choices to the youth in my constituency. Most of them have to go to distant places to pursue higher studies or some professional course. It is time the villages are connected to the urban areas and there is a healthy sharing of profits. That's the only way we can surge ahead.

BRING IN TOURISTS

A reputed international agency, the World Travel and Tourism Council, states that India will be a tourist hotspot from 2009–2018, with a ten-year high-growth potential. Presently, tourism contributes 6.23 per cent to the national GDP and 8.78 per cent of the total employment in the country. Yet, the focus on this sector is lopsided. Just a few states or regions have been allowed to grow. As a 5,000-year-old civilisation, which is culturally, religiously and historically so rich, India has a lot to show. But lack of infrastructure has prevented tourism from reaching its true potential. A good example is one of the districts, Deogarh, in Jharkhand, which is an important pilgrimage centre for the Hindus. It is one of the fifty-one Shakti Peethas and, as a result, receives a huge number of pilgrims. About 50 million people visited the place in 2012. Karna, a mythological character from the Mahabharata, is believed to be from this place. Moreover, the Mandar hill, which according to Hindu mythology was used by the gods to churn the ocean to fetch life-giving nectar, can be found in this region. In Champapuri are two important pilgrimage centres of the Jains. These examples are just to enunciate the kind of history these small places boast of and how they can be developed as major religious tourist centres. All one needs is rail and airport connectivity and world-class infrastructure to attract international tourists.

I am proud to say that I represent a constituency which is religiously, historically and ecologically so rich. That's all the more reason why I feel that such places need to be developed and their true potential as tourist hubs have to be realised.

WORKING ON SKILLS

For inclusive growth, it's essential to provide sustainable livelihoods to people. And for that, developing skills is the first step. India has the world's youngest workforce—over half of the population is below 25 years and various studies cite that by 2020 the average age will be 29, compared with China's 37 years. At the same time, the global economy will witness a shortage of skilled manpower to the extent of around 56 million. A 2010 study conducted by the international investment banking firm Goldman Sachs found that a demographically young India will be the largest contributor to the global labour force in the coming decades. It also stated that India will add nearly 110 million workers by 2020. In contrast, China's labour force will increase by 15 million while Japan's labour force will decline by 3 million. In such a scenario, the government has to step up its skill development programme. The focus should now shift towards courses which can generate employment, such as civil construction, electrical, hospitality etc. in order to meet the growing demand. More ITIs and polytechnics should be opened in semi-urban and rural India. Such a move will have a twin effect—the youth will get employment opportunities and more people can be lifted out of poverty. The government, in the wake of the growing demand, launched a National Skill Development Mission in 2008 consisting of three institutions. These are the National Council on Skill Development for policy direction, the National Skill Development Coordination Board to enumerate strategies required to implement the decisions of the PM's council and the National

Skill Development Corporation, a non-profit organisation which is expected to meet the skill training requirements of the labour market including the unorganised sector. This is fine, but more emphasis has to be laid on skill-developing courses across all the states. Developing the right skills and thus, providing an opportunity for employment, can be one of the many ways of making India's population its asset. China has done it and so can we.

HEALTH MATTERS

A Planning Commission report of 2008 stated that India is short of 600,000 doctors, one million nurses and 200,000 dental surgeons. What is worse, as per the Health Ministry statistics of 2009, is that rural India is short of 16,000 doctors including 12,000 specialists. And this shortage is most acute in the villages of Uttar Pradesh and Madhya Pradesh. If corrective measures are not taken immediately, rural healthcare will be in a shambles. The National Rural Health Mission (NRHM) has been trying to address this shocking disconnect but so far, not much has been achieved. In itself, NRHM is a good project which is doing some excellent work at the grass-roots level. It is a sad state of affairs that the medical doctors refuse to work in villages. Part of the reason is the lack of basic infrastructure in rural India. The other major reason is the poor salary. If these can be addressed, then there is no reason why doctors will not be attracted to serve in rural India. The government should bring in a law that makes it mandatory for doctors to work in the villages for a few years. Lack of doctors is not the only problem plaguing rural India. A severe shortage of good hospitals is a reality. Not all villages have health centres and hospitals. And even if they are there, then the most basic equipment and facilities would be missing. After six decades of Independence, access to quality and affordable healthcare remains a dream. We need to change that with immediate effect.

The government should make it mandatory to build hospitals in villages with a population of over 100,000. These hospitals should be equipped with all the necessary medical equipment. The other important step would be to increase the number of medical colleges in rural India, particularly in north, central and northeastern India. The South, however, has a concentration of nearly 80 per cent of India's medical and nursing colleges. As a result, access to basic healthcare facilities is far better in the southern states. Tamil Nadu is a good example, with its focus on State-funded primary healthcare. Maybe that can be replicated in other states. We need to have uniformity in healthcare across states.

STOP INFILTRATION

This is one issue which needs to be addressed urgently. Illegal immigration into India is becoming a curse for the nation. The largest chunk of infiltration happens from Bangladesh. India shares a 2,429-mile-long border with its eastern neighbour and most of it is not managed well, leading to illegal crossovers on a daily basis. Though no reliable data is available on the number of illegal Bangladeshi migrants in India, the 2001 Census figures peg the number at 2 million. It could definitely be much more. Most of the infiltrators go to West Bengal and the northeastern states. In Assam, agitation started against the infiltrators way back in 1979, led by the All Assam Students Union. More recently, the Shiv Sena has protested against the Bangladeshi infiltrators in Mumbai. The problem is that they are rapidly spreading out to different parts of India—of late, moving to Kerala—without any way of checking their movement. Most of them manage to get a ration card and eventually acquire Indian citizenship, thus making it difficult for authorities to deport them. We should not look at these illegal infiltrators from a religious angle; we should simply address the issue of infiltration which is a huge burden on the country's economy. We need to manage our borders better by strengthening and expanding the electrical fence programme; raising more battalions of the border security forces and developing infrastructure (building roads) in the border regions.

India's porous international borders have made it a safe conduit for all kinds of nefarious activities. From smuggling of arms, narcotics and fake currency into India to human trafficking, the porous borders with Nepal, China and Myanmar are largely giving rise to criminal activities, particularly the border with Nepal which has helped in creating the 'Red Corridor' or the areas where Maoists are most active. These include states such as Bihar, Chhattisgarh, Odisha, Andhra Pradesh, Jharkhand, West Bengal, Uttar Pradesh and Madhya Pradesh, and now this movement is moving towards Gujarat and Maharashtra. The eastern states were economically weak and hence, easily came under Maoist influence. Also, these States are the richest in minerals and the spread of Maoist activities has made it difficult for sourcing the minerals. One has to remember that the aim of the Maoists is to destabilise the Indian state and push India's economic development on the back foot. These are serious internal security issues and have to be controlled soon if India wants to become a developed nation. To tackle the problem of Naxalism, terrorism and insurgency—the three security nightmares of modern India—a comprehensive policy has to be mooted. Stricter law enforcement and proactive policies aimed at development of core infrastructure as well as soft infrastructure including healthcare and education are the answers to tackle this menace.

Conclusion

After all these years, when India is on the right path—to reclaim its lost glory of being a superpower—the government should pull out all stops to help it achieve its goal. By building the right infrastructure, providing quality healthcare to all and tackling threats to the country's security, the government can bring the two Indias closer. Let there be only one Bharat, the one the whole world will look up to. I gave up a career in the corporate world—I was a director in Essar—to contribute to India's growth and I am confident that in the next decade or so, we will realise the dream of becoming a truly developed nation.

ೠಌ

Poonamben Veljibhai Jat

A first-time Member of Parliament from Kutch, Poonamben Veljibhai Jat beat 16 other candidates, including three other women, to win her seat in 2009.

Born in 1971, Poonamben Jat is a member of the Bharatiya Janata Party (BJP). She began her journey as a party worker in Mumbai, before entering active politics in Gandhidham, Gujarat, where she contested and won the municipal elections in 2000. She is a vocal spokesperson on gender issues, having begun her political journey with the women's wing of the party.

She has represented India at several international conferences such as in the Commonwealth countries parliamentary seminars in the year 2009 in the UK and Europe, and was a member of the BJP team that went to USA for developing better ties with the Republication Party, in the year 2011. She is presently the Vice-president of the Indo-Oman Parliamentary Group, and Member of the Parliamentary Forum for Scheduled Castes and Scheduled Tribes and the Parliamentary Forum for Youth.

INDIA

Sorry, Sir—I can't afford an election again!
The last time I won—and I couldn't recover
even half the investment!

Towards Self-sufficiency

Poonamben Veljibhai Jat

> The model for evaluating growth and development in India should be changed from GDP (Gross Domestic Product) and GNP (Gross National Product) to HDI (Human Development Index). This will ensure that the government monitors not only the total quantity of goods and services produced in India but also the quality of the standard of living that Indians have.

For someone who doesn't come from a political family and was just a party worker in Mumbai, becoming a parliamentarian is a great honour. The Indian Parliament is the seat of the world's largest democracy. And I am proud to be a member of this Parliament. Both politically and economically, India is going through an interesting phase and it gives me immense joy to be able to contribute in nation-building at this point.

The world looks at India in awe and with great hope. In the last fifteen years, the Indian economy has grown and led to a boom in various sectors, particularly services, telecom and retail. Foreign investors are keen to invest here. Most international companies want to have a presence in India. It is at this critical juncture that we need to introspect; accept the many drawbacks that India suffers from and find a way forward, for only then will India realise its true potential.

Let's look at some issues which, if addressed immediately and intelligently, will solve the country's problems.

CORRUPTION

Corruption in politics bothers me. It is so deeply embedded in the system that few people want to take up politics as a career option. In order to attract good and honest people, the first step should be to make the process of funding for elections much more transparent. It is quite natural that the people, who use a few crores to contest an election, will try to recover that amount—maybe more—once elected. And they can do this only through wrong means. Moreover, there will be political favours to be returned, and the ways for doing so may not always be righteous. To tackle this menace, new reforms and strict rules have to be implemented by the Election Commission (EC). There should be a strict vigil on how the money is being sourced and later used, with a special focus on constituencies which have had cases of money laundering. Fund collection and expenditure by parties should be made more systematic and transparent. We are living in the most technologically advanced times when it is not at all difficult to find out about corrupt practices. So, if we utilise technology to our advantage, curbing corruption will not be difficult. In fact, all the funds collected should be accounted for. Also, if elections are made less expensive, candidates wouldn't opt for unfair means to secure funds.

What also stops most people from joining politics is the presence of candidates with criminal records. The EC has taken steps in the past to prevent this, and should continue to do so more firmly. Only then will good people come in and bring in new ideas about governance—much required in this age.

All the major developing sectors like industry, information and technology, aviation, shipping and agriculture need to be free from corruption. More importantly, the ruling party, the opposition and the bureaucracy should all work together for the development of our nation. The judiciary should also be empowered to deal strictly with those found guilty of corruption and the whole judicial process should be swift and without loopholes.

AGRICULTURE

In the days of the monarchs, good governance meant making more jobs available to the people so that they could live a better life. So, even during famines, kings used to build palaces and temples so that people could have jobs and could earn money. But now, nobody bothers and as a result, people suffer. Agriculture is the mainstay of the Indian economy and employs 52 per cent of India's workforce. It would make perfect sense to give a boost to this sector so that more employment and revenue is generated. The contribution of agriculture to the overall GDP has shrunk to about 14 per cent, which is said to be a trend in the process of development of any economy. But even then, a growth rate of 2 per cent in agriculture is abysmally low for a developing country. This has been the scenario for the last ten years. As a result of this, the economy has grown at a lower rate. To increase the growth, a second green revolution is necessary. For that it's imperative to invest in research and development so that better results are achieved. This is the best way forward to ensure that farmers get employment, and that there is an increase in their purchasing power. Perhaps a lesson can be learnt from Gujarat which has been contributing 11 per cent to the 2 per cent of India's agricultural growth.

Another major setback to the agricultural sector is the delay in various irrigation projects. While a lot of irrigation projects have been commissioned in various parts of the country and work on many has begun, an inordinate amount of time is being spent to complete them. As a result, the cost of the project multiplies. This is clearly a waste of the taxpayer's money. Look at what is happening to irrigation projects, in the districts of Maharashtra, where large amounts have been spent without any apparent results. So, it is extremely important that irrigation projects of building dams and canals, are not delayed and are executed on time to increase the productivity of agricultural land.

When it comes to milk production, India continues to be the largest milk producing nation in the world with close to 17 per cent of the global production, according to the National Dairy Development Board (NDDB). It is also the largest consumer of milk in the world. In fact, *The Indian Express*, dated 17 August 2012, quoted the government to report that during the 2011-12 fiscal, the compounded annual growth rate of milk production was higher compared to the growth of population in the past one year. This is definitely great news but we should not rest on our laurels. It is time we brought in a second White Revolution. The seventies brought in Operation Flood (White Revolution), which transformed a milk-deficient country into the largest milk-producing nation in the world. Now we should take it a step further and try to solve our malnutrition problem to a large extent through surplus production. I want to cite the example of Gujarat, how we are aiming to tackle malnutrition by making milk freely available to children. Chief Minister Narendra Modi suggested that at the time of collection of milk, a part of it should be kept aside for Anganwadi children. All Gram Samitis have been asked to do so. This ensures that Anganwadi children get to drink milk every day. The Chief Minister has also mooted the idea that party workers should celebrate their and their families' birthdays and anniversaries by sending sweets and fruits to Anganwadi children. Once again this ensures that the Anganwadi children get regular nutrition. If this idea is implemented all over India, malnutrition among children can actually be controlled.

Agriculture in India has the potential for larger productivity than its present level. But our poor infrastructure prevents it from achieving this potential. Take for example the fact that India is the second largest producer of fruit and vegetables. Yet, not all of it reaches the consumer; at least 30-35 per cent perishes in transit. The solution to this serious problem lies in building chains of cold storages on farms and fields. This will ensure that the vegetables and fruits do not perish and are available for consumption at a cheaper price. This measure will again be a step in reducing malnourishment.

EDUCATION

Both education and health need much more attention from the government than what's given to them at present. This is all the more important in order to meet the Millennium Development Goals (MDG) set by the United Nations. A major problem that India faces is illiteracy. The Census of India 2011 statistics show that in the last ten years there has been an improvement—literacy rates have gone up by almost 9 per cent. In 2001, the literacy figures were 65.38 per cent and in 2012, they increased to 74.04 per cent—the ground reality remains more or less the same. In villages, children continue to drop out of schools and despite the Right to Education (RTE) Act, which makes education free and compulsory for children in the age group 6-14, a large number of children still don't have access to education. So, first and foremost, it is vital that a concerted effort is made to ensure that children in the villages go to school regularly. It's in the rural areas that most children drop out after a few years, especially girls. Schools have to be made more attractive and some sort of incentive should be given so that parents send their children regularly to school. Once this is overcome, our next challenge would be to make education more practical and skill-oriented. More vocational courses should be provided so that students are able to get a job once they complete the course. Also, computer education should be introduced in all village schools so that students are in step with the latest technology. Another opportunity that should be given to the students is to choose sports as a career. The government can look at building sports universities so that youngsters are encouraged to take up sports. In Gujarat, we have already started the initiative to build sports universities; an example the rest of the country can follow. Primarily, we have to eradicate illiteracy and link education to employment. That's important to attain the status of a superpower.

Health is another major concern. Sadly, India spends about 1 per cent of its GDP on healthcare. Health is a primary responsibility of the government as it is wedded to the idea of social welfare. But despite its best efforts, the government has not been successful in providing healthcare to all. That's why it is important that a public-private partnership model should be adopted to address healthcare issues in the country.

HUMAN DEVELOPMENT INDEX

The model for evaluating growth and development in India should be changed from GDP (Gross Domestic Product) and GNP (Gross National Product) to HDI (Human Development Index). This will ensure that the government monitors not only the total quantity of goods and services produced in India but also the quality of the standard of living that Indians have.

The growth has to be necessarily inclusive, which means that the wealth created by a high rate of GDP growth should be equally distributed among all strata of society. Also, subsidies should not be wiped out as a large number of people live below the poverty line in India. Instead, a more efficient delivery system for the subsidies has to be evolved. One way could be by depositing cash directly to the bank account of the woman head of the beneficiary family.

NUCLEAR ENERGY

India's power demands are growing every year, a fact that became shockingly evident in 2012 when almost half of the nation was plunged into darkness due to a power grid failure. The solution to a problem like this is to implement our nuclear power programme in full. Nuclear energy is the future and India hopes to supply 25 per cent of electricity from nuclear power by 2050. Nuclear power is one of the safest methods of producing energy. As per the International Atomic Energy Agency (IAEA) Report, India possesses two-thirds (67 per cent) of the world's reserve of monazite, the primary ore of thorium. So when we have thorium, we shouldn't hesitate to go ahead with our nuclear power programme. In fact, India should also concentrate on utilising other natural resources like wind and solar. New research centres should be opened which would focus on developing technology for utilising the natural resources to the maximum. All states must work in unison to make India a power-efficient country. Gujarat is self-sufficient in power, and that's one of the reasons why industries are willing to invest in the State. Gujarat gets a lot of its power from renewable energy sources such as solar and wind. In Kutch, the constituency that I represent and which is close to the sea, we have signed MoUs with other countries to generate power from tides. So if we can do it, then other states can also look at alternate sources of power generation. My vision is to see India sell power to the world and for that, we have to invest in clean energy.

WOMEN'S ISSUES

Women's empowerment should not be on paper alone but should be seen on ground. The reality is much different from what is generally perceived. Despite reservations, in governance, women are not able to come forward in large numbers. Men continue to oppose representation of women in public offices. The only way women will get an equal opportunity to perform in public life will be when every political party has, out of its own choice, women candidates. This should not be a compulsion, rather parties should willingly bring in more women to the fore. Today, more women are educated than before and so they should be given the opportunity to have a say in different spheres of public life. There should be more job opportunities for them, easy loans and subsidies for women entrepreneurs and reforms in laws to make it safe for them to work. Unless the right environment is created, women will not come forward.

Here, I want to share an incident that showcases the strength and determination of Kutchi women. During the 1972 Indo-Pakistan war, the Air Force's border airport was bombarded and completely destroyed. It was crucial for the airport to be back in function. So the Air Force commander called the villagers of Madhapur to rebuild the airport. Now, this village had only women, as the men worked in smaller towns outside Kutch. Time was limited and there was no other option. The women, however, were confident that they could do the job. And they did. In one night, they rebuilt the entire airport. I have cited this example to highlight the fact that if women are given an opportunity, they can tackle problems much more intelligently and systematically.

As a young parliamentarian, I think a lot of responsibility lies on my shoulders. I never dreamt of being in a public position. I was satisfied being a party worker with the Bharatiya Janata Party in Mumbai. Later, when I started living in Kutch after my marriage, I took the plunge into active politics. In 2000, I contested the municipal elections from Gandhidham municipality. I won with a good margin and became a councillor. That was a turning point in my life as it exposed me to nation-building, albeit at a very primary stage. The second turning point was when the Chief Minister invited me to contest the Lok Sabha seat from Kutch—the largest constituency in the country. Once again, I won with a thumping majority in 2009 and became an MP at 37. Three years in Parliament is a short time to bring about the desired changes but when I look back, I can proudly say that I have managed to get some work done in Kutch. The construction of a road connecting Santalpur with Gadhuli, pending for the last twenty-seven years owing to environmental clearances (it passed through an animal sanctuary), was completed after I spoke with former Environment Minister Jairam Ramesh. The road, connecting Ahmedabad to the border, is vital for the development of Kutch as well as for the security of the nation. It is the shortest route to Ahmedabad from Kutch. In addition, I brought twelve trains to Kutch and Morbi. Also, we have completed the vessel traffic management system for the ports—Kandla and Mundra—which had been pending for the last seven years. This is vital for the security of the country.

When I walk through the hallowed portals of Parliament, I am filled with pride. My years in Parliament and my travels abroad as a Lok Sabha member have taught me a lot. Most importantly, it has taught me that if all the elected representatives of the people work together, there is no reason why we can't make India a superpower. I do not believe in the word 'impossible'. Everything is possible with a positive attitude and approach in life. We won freedom from foreign rulers because of this attitude, and we can once again, overcome our shortcomings and achieve greatness.

ॐ

Priya Dutt Roncon

Priya Dutt Roncon is an Indian National Congress
Member of Parliament from the Mumbai North West
constituency, since 2004.

Born in 1966, Dutt studied in Sophia College, Mumbai
and The Center For Media Arts, New York, and dabbled in the
entertainment industry in production and editing before she
found her calling and joined the Spastic Society of India as
trustee. She headed the department of policy change in the
institution to promote inclusive education. She joined
politics after the demise of her father, Sunil Dutt. She
is vocal on issues of children and women's rights.

She says her ambition in life is to be decent. 'Decent in the
way I live my life, in the work I do, and with the people I meet.
It is this belief that I will always keep closest to my heart, and
use it as my guide in every decision I make.'

She is a certified scuba diver and sports enthusiast, and has
repeatedly talked about the importance of sports in a young,
growing nation. A writer and an animal lover, she penned a
memoir about her celebrity parents and continues to work
for the charitable trust set up in the memory of her mother,
the Nargis Dutt Mobile Hospital for the poor.

INDIA

How I miss the old times when you had to wait
for years to get a phone connection!

Let's Not Make it So Grim

PRIYA DUTT RONCON

> When I look around and see scores of women and young girls who refuse to be threatened or silenced by societal norms, I know there is hope. I believe it is women like these who will bring about the change in India. Education has given them the confidence and awareness to fight for their rights and in the process they will fight for the rights of millions of other women and children.

Six decades is a long time in a nation's history. For a newly independent India in 1947, the road ahead must have seemed full of challenges. Yet, these challenges spurred the nation-builders on as they went about putting India on the world map. Sixty years on, India has grown in strength and achieved much. Today, it is an IT major and an economic powerhouse that the world cannot ignore.

India is a land of diversity, a rainbow of different cultures, traditions, languages and religions. Our natural resources and self-reliability in many areas set us apart from many western and Asian countries. Over the last two decades, a lot has changed in the country. The IT and telecom revolution has brought in major changes and put India on a fast-track to growth. Yet, it is disheartening to see India lag behind on many social parameters. Health, education and status of women and children are some of the major areas that need immediate intervention. Great efforts are being made by the government where the main thrust has been inclusive growth. But much more needs to be done.

I believe that the pillars of a progressive nation are health and education, and these are the pillars that need to be strengthened if we truly want to see inclusive growth. As a young parliamentarian, I dream of an India where every child has access to quality education and affordable healthcare; where the girl child is not killed even before she is born; where a woman doesn't suffer the indignities one cannot even imagine and where children don't know what hunger is.

To achieve this, first and foremost, we need to address the issues of population growth and control. As per the Census 2011 statistics, we are a nation of 1.22 billion people. Of this, 628.8 million are men and 591.4 women. The sex ratio is 940 females per 1,000 males. Around 50 per cent of the population is in the age group of 0-25. It is estimated that by the end of 2030, India will have a population of 1.53 billion, surpassing China, which is the most populated country in the world today. In many respects our population can become our advantage. We will have a large pool of talent and potential workforce, but this is possible only if we educate and train this captive workforce.

EDUCATION

Various efforts have been made to improve the country's primary education. Yet, they have not yielded the kind of result one would have expected. At 74.04 per cent, India's literacy rate is way below the world average of 84 per cent. It has the largest illiterate population in the world. If India wishes to be counted among the leading economies of the world, it has to overcome the challenge of illiteracy. And this has to be done on a war-footing. Without education, India can never realise its dream.

The year 2009 was historic. That year the Right to Education Act (RTE) was passed. Nearly 60 years after the Constitution mandated that education to children between 6-14 years should be free and compulsory, it became a reality. Education may be a fundamental right now but it will be some years before it truly becomes one.

To ensure RTE is implemented for what it truly stands for, we should not just concentrate on numbers, but also on the quality of education. And for that, infrastructure, teaching staff and facilities have to improve across the nation in our public school system. The kind of education that a child receives in Kerala, for example, should be available to a child in a rural area in the Northeast. We can definitely do this; we just need the determination and dedication. Standardisation of education is very important. In the US, for example, public schools across the country have the same standard of education and majority of the children there go to public schools. It is imperative to strengthen our public education system and ensure that not just a small percentage of children but the majority have access to quality education.

As we try to address our elementary education problems, we should also pay heed to our secondary education. None of our universities rank among the top ones. In the 2012 QS World University Rankings, not a single Indian university figured in the top 200. In 2010, the London-based Times Higher Education (THE) Rankings, considered the gold standard for international university rankings, rated 27 Asian universities in the world's top 200. Not a single was from India. Rather, China had six on the list. It is indeed a shame, given that once India was a respected seat of learning and institutions like Nalanda were famous all over the world. Today, we are focussed on adding more universities, unconcerned about the quality. China, on the other hand, is focussed on building universities which can compete with the best in the world. As a knowledge-based economy, we have to invest in world-class universities.

This thought was also conveyed by Prime Minister Manmohan Singh when he spoke at the golden jubilee convocation of IIT Bombay in 2012. "Every year when I see how many hundreds of thousands of students apply for admission to these institutions, and when I see how high have become the minimum cut-off marks for admission, my heart is pained by the limits we are placing on the opportunities available to our youth.' He also said, 'As India's economy becomes bigger and more developed, so too must our knowledge base. A developing country like ours has to catch up with other more developed nations and this 'catch-up' process depends vitally on our ability to harness human resources for development. Another challenge is to ensure that the investment we make in higher education, in fact, contributes more directly to nation-building."

It is all the more important why our education should be focussed on developing skills. India's population is a constant worry for policymakers. And with an unemployment rate of 9.4 per cent, it is a challenge for the government to create jobs. As a result, it should be our focus to develop skills and introduce the youth to vocational training programmes so that they don't have to necessarily depend on others for employment. In this way, we will empower them with the right training so that they can create wealth as well as sustain themselves.

Unfortunately, what holds our education system back is the quota policy. I personally have my reservations about 'reservations' in the name of caste. The quota system, which has been introduced in higher education, is taking the country back by a few steps as we ignore merit. Instead, let all children be given free and quality education under the RTE Act—this is the first step to an inclusive society. This will ensure that at the primary level, children receive good education and eventually, reach a level where they can be competitive. Then at the college level, let merit decide, and not quota. If deserving and meritorious students make it to our hallowed institutions such as the IITs and IIMs, we can rest assured that they will produce the best minds and contribute to the growth of the country; thus, echoing the dreams of our prime minister.

Let's not forget what Jawaharlal Nehru once said when addressing the Constituent Assembly in May 1949, 'I try to look upon the problem not in the sense of religious minority, but rather in the sense of helping backward groups in the country. I do not look at it from a religious point of view or a caste point of view, but from the point of view that a backward group ought to be helped and I am glad that this reservation will be limited to ten years...'

In 1949, reservation was brought in to boost and help the backward groups to reach a level from where they could compete equally. It was supposed to be a temporary solution, limited to ten years. But now it seems to have become a permanent solution.

I firmly believe in the saying: 'Don't give them fish, rather teach them to fish'.

HEALTH

It's a sad contradiction. On the one hand, we are an economy to reckon with, and on the other, we have one of the worst rates in malnutrition. The 2011 Global Hunger Index (GHI) Report placed India 15th among leading countries with a hunger problem. As per the World Bank, India ranks second in the world for malnutrition among children. The government has been trying to work on this problem but the challenges are too many. Population and illiteracy are the two main challenges. And this is not just a problem of the rural poor, even urban poor face severe malnutrition. I represent a constituency, Mumbai North Central, which is part of the financial capital of the country. It could not be more ironical that the city where money rules, is home to innumerable slums, including Asia's largest slum, Dharavi.

Increase in population over the years has also resulted in slum population growth. Mumbai is home to an estimated 6.5 million slum dwellers. Nearly 55 per cent of the city's population lives in slums. Despite government efforts to build new houses and other basic infrastructure, most of the slum residents do not have basic civic amenities like toilets and clean water. Therefore, lack of hygiene results in health problems. My constituency has nearly 70 per cent of slums and health is a major cause of worry here. There are three municipal hospitals which are not enough to cater to the demand. We have been conducting regular awareness drives on hygiene and health. But that's not enough. Hopefully, urban health issues will be addressed through the National Urban Health Mission, which is being launched to encompass the primary healthcare needs of people in the urban areas.

In the last few decades, various deadly diseases have become common in India. HIV, cancer, heart ailments, renal failures, thalassemia are just some of them. For all these and more we require early diagnosis and treatment, but for that we need enough doctors, nurses and diagnostic centres. We severely lack doctors, nurses and medical aid for the ever-growing population. Union Health and Family Welfare Minister Ghulam Nabi Azad said in 2012 that India faces a shortage of 1 million MBBS doctors. And this severe shortage is affecting delivery of healthcare in rural India.

Cancer is one of the diseases which require early diagnosis. And unfortunately, we don't have enough trained personnel or diagnostic centres to detect it. The fight against cancer is one which I have been associated with for a long time now. It's a personal fight at one level—my mother, actor Nargis Dutt, died of the disease. More than two decades later, the incidences of cancer cases in India have not come down. A new study published in *The Lancet* (dated 28 March 2012) reported that 555,000 people died of cancer in 2010. Tobacco-related cancer deaths in men was around 42 per cent while cervical, stomach and breast cancers accounted for 41 per cent of cancer deaths in women. India has the highest cases of head and neck cancer among men and cervical and breast cancers in women. The numbers are growing every day.

The World Health Organization reports that deaths from cancer worldwide are projected to continue rising, with an estimated 12 million deaths in 2030. In 2008, more than 70 per cent of all cancer deaths occurred in low- and middle-income countries.

The concept of 'Healthcare for All' was emphasized in a white paper released by Hosmac, a healthcare and hospital consultancy, and the Federation of Indian Chambers of Commerce and Industry (FICCI) in 2010. In addition, some interesting facts were brought to the fore. The government's share of expenditure on health is just 26 per cent, the remaining 74 per cent is spent by private players. Private health facilities proliferate where people can pay. The challenge is, therefore, to develop a healthcare delivery system that overcomes this inequality, and is available, accessible and affordable to all. According to the white paper, India has a very low hospital bed density of 0.9 per thousand people which is less than the norm of three beds per thousand people as laid down by WHO. In rural areas, a population of 30,000 has a primary health centre of only four to six beds. In the sample studied, it was revealed that India has the highest number of medical colleges but the lowest number of doctors per thousand people in the sample studied. It also has the lowest number of nurses per thousand people. All these make availability of adequate and appropriate healthcare a serious problem.

WOMEN AND CHILDREN

Like health and education, women and children are of great importance to a nation. As they say, if you educate a woman, you are educating the entire family. A healthy woman translates into a healthy family. Unfortunately in India, both education and health are elusive to the woman. In most cases, girls are not allowed to study and if they are, then the drop-out rate is high. It is estimated that more than 245 million Indian women lack the basic ability to read and write. In 2012, literacy rates for men were 82.14 per cent and for women 65.45 per cent. When it comes to health, once again they are neglected. As per United Nations figures, India accounted for a third of maternal deaths globally in 2010. India shares this sad distinction with Nigeria. The story is the same when it comes to rape cases—India stands fourth, behind countries like Sri Lanka, Jordan and Argentina. The picture that one gets of women in India is pretty dismal and also contradictory. On the one hand, women are treated so poorly and on the other, India has had some prominent women personalities. And even today, whether it is politics, films, education or the corporate world, we have some powerful ladies reigning at the top. What's more, in India Hindus worship the woman as Shakti— we have an array of goddesses. Yet, every day, every hour, some woman is either getting raped, abused, dying in childbirth or being killed for dowry. It's now routine to see reports in the newspapers stating how India is the most unsafe place to be born a woman. This is indeed pitiable. How have we come to such a state where the world points an accusatory finger at us? Of course, a lot has to do with our social conditioning and the patriarchal system. The mindsets will take a few more centuries to change but the efforts being made are noteworthy. Under the government's National Rural Health Mission (NRHM), a trained female community health worker or Accredited Social Health Activist (ASHA) has been assigned to every village. It's her responsibility to create awareness about various health problems and also counsel on preparing for childbirth. So far, the concept has worked and some good amount of work has been done at the ground level. But a lot needs to be done still. The government has been working towards empowering women and one of the steps is by supporting and creating self-help groups to make women financially independent. Another progressive step has been providing reservation for women in the panchayats. Also, the 50 per cent reservation for women in the local corporation elections has given them an opportunity to be part of the political process. This participation of women in the legislature will bring about a big change in their status.

Children play a crucial role in the growth of a nation—they are its future. But this subject, I feel, has not been given due importance in Parliament. Even the budget allocation for issues dealing with children is not enough. According to the report brought out by HAQ Centre for Child Rights in 2011, 5.3 per cent of the Union Budget is Budget for Children (BFC) with an increase of 0.3 per cent since 2011-12. This must be set against the inflation rate of 6.6 per cent. I also feel that there should be a separate ministry for child welfare in order to give undivided attention to the future citizens of the nation. At about 400 million, India has the world's largest child population. We as a country are the worst in the way we treat our children. Whether it's child marriage, child labour or child abuse, it all thrives in India. At one point of time, Goa earned the shocking distinction of being India's paedophile capital. A report by UNICEF states that there are some 17 million child workers in the country, the highest in the world. About 12 per cent, between the ages 5-14, are engaged in child labour activities. Despite a Child Labour (Prohibition & Regulation) Act introduced in 1986, children under

14 years can still be found working, some even engaged in menial activities. When it comes to their health, the picture is even more dismal. As per the United Nations, 2.1 million children die before the age of five, mostly from preventable diseases such as diarrhoea, typhoid, measles and malaria. And over 900,000 newborns die every year before turning a month old, says a study conducted by experts at the World Health Organization, Save the Children and the London School of Hygiene and Tropical Medicine, which was published in 2011. It revealed that two-thirds of children are victims of physical abuse; over 50 per cent face some kind of sexual abuse while half of the children face emotional abuse.

What is equally bad is that 4 per cent of our population comprises orphaned or abandoned children, who have no future and are in many ways invisible. They have no identification, no paperwork to support their future and thus, are unable to get school admissions or avail any other facilities. They walk the streets, exploited both physically and sexually by faceless people. Their lives are snuffed out even before they reach adulthood. And these innocent lives end up to become subjects of documentaries, which win accolades at international film festivals, watched by thousands in the comforts of their living rooms.

The most heinous crime in my eyes is child abuse and deserves the severest of punishment.

We are living in the twenty-first century but all these statistics make one feel as if the Dark Ages still continue. Unless stricter laws are brought in and severe punishment handed out to the culprits, the status of Indian children will not change. We have to wake up immediately and take action; after all, the future of the country rests on these tiny shoulders. We have to strengthen them with love, respect and confidence. A nation which does not take care of its women and children cannot be called developed, not in the least on the social index.

After eight years in Parliament, I have realised that things can change with timely minor interventions. They can create large impacts and I have seen this happen. Also important to bring in change is to have synergy between civil society and elected representatives. The latter have the mandate to bring about change but they cannot work in isolation. Together with civil society they can make the change happen. We have laws against various social evils such as dowry, female foeticide, child labour, protection of children against abuse, protection of women against rape and molestation and so on and so forth. But implementation of these laws is virtually non-existent. We must have a mechanism to ensure the implementation of these laws. In a population of 1.22 billion we still lack manpower, whether it is in the medical field, the police force or the judiciary. This needs to be addressed immediately.

When I look around and see scores of women and young girls who refuse to be threatened or silenced by societal norms, I know there is hope. I am greatly inspired by stories of people like activist Flavia Agnes, who escaped an abusive marriage, educated herself to become a lawyer and now fights for the rights of women; Olympic winner Mary Kom, a farm labourer's daughter who fought all hardships including threat from insurgents in Manipur, to emerge as a world boxing champion; my cook's young daughter who refused to marry the guy chosen by her parents because he asked for dowry. There are countless such instances around us, and I believe it is women like these who will bring about the change in India. Education has given them the confidence and awareness to fight for their rights and in the process they will fight for the rights of millions of other women and children.

It's these unsung heroes who will take us to the next level. We just need to join hands with them and give them the best opportunity.

౷౦౷

Sanjay Jaiswal

A Member of Parliament from the constituency of Paschim Champaran in Bihar, Sanjay Jaiswal belongs to the Bharatiya Janata Party (BJP).

Born in 1965, Jaiswal is a doctor specializing in general medicine and is national in-charge of the BJP medical cell. He is deeply engaged with issues related to healthcare, and believes that it should be at the top of the nation's political agenda. Making healthcare accessible and available is one of his chief concerns, and as a qualified medical practitioner, he brings a unique level of knowledge and dedication to his work. Jaiswal is also involved with the idea of a clean, green India. He has supported the development of affordable and easily-available biofuels and other renewable sources of energy.

Fond of badminton and swimming, he has written a scientific thesis and book on the role of micronutrients and minerals in overcoming myocardial infarction.

INDIA

What? Has the petrol price gone up again?!

Looking at a
Greener Future

SANJAY JAISWAL

> I firmly believe that renewable energy can solve the problems
> of India in many ways—not only could it build energy security
> by tapping on our diverse resources and reducing our import
> dependence, but it could also be successfully deployed in areas and
> sectors which are seriously lagging behind.

All Indians dream of their nation being successful and developed. It's a dream of a nation where the basic necessities of life are met; where people don't go hungry; where corruption doesn't exist; where each citizen is able to live with dignity; where women and children are treated with respect; where peace reigns—it may sound utopian but it's the dream of every citizen. And as a citizen and a parliamentarian, I too have the same dream. India, I know, is passing through an interesting phase—its high-growth-rate economy has now been challenged, necessitating bold policy reforms and their timely implementation. And at this crucial juncture of nation-building, the people of India rightfully expect us parliamentarians to bring in those reforms.

Development doesn't simply mean building roads and houses. It is about lifting the poor out of poverty and giving them options of a better life. It is also about bridging the rural and urban divide to bring in holistic development. And at the same time, it is about eradicating social evils like dowry and female foeticide, wiping out malnutrition and infant mortality, saving the farmers from committing suicide and saving the environment from getting degraded further. The government has been trying to effect major changes through various projects. The National Rural Health Mission (NRHM) is one such project that is expected to change the idea of quality healthcare in rural areas. This is one project which has the bipartisan support of parliamentarians for large public investment for the Mission. But so far, the Mission's appraisals haven't been encouraging. Alleged corruption and malpractices in some states have shaken public confidence in this noble Mission. As a remedy, the design of the Mission needs a radical change—one that would usher greater public-private synergy which in turn would mobilise more private resources with each unit of public investment. Similarly, the Mahatma Gandhi National Rural Employment Guarantee Act (MGNREGA) is a good scheme launched to provide guaranteed employment in rural areas. But if it has to be really successful in building a new India, it has to be linked to skill development and upgraded quality of work. We cannot let our rural folk be earth-diggers forever! These are just two of the many examples that I feel can make a difference, if implemented a little differently.

A decade is not too far away in a nation's life. But if the work is done with dedication and sincerity, the goal of becoming a developed nation in ten years, can be achieved easily. Then, it's not tough to dream of India as a manufacturing hub, especially in electronics, and a leader in the pharmaceutical industry. I would also like to see India emerge as a frontrunner in the use of clean energy sources.

Let's look at some of the crucial sectors which need immediate action.

NUTS AND BOLTS

India's manufacturing sector has been contributing about 14 per cent to the Gross Domestic Product (GDP). The recently launched National Manufacturing Policy aims to enhance the share of manufacturing in the GDP to 25 per cent within a decade. That's indeed an ambitious plan. It is still a long way ahead. While automobiles, consumer durables to engineering products are being manufactured by MNCs in India, not much is being done in the field of electronics. Let's not forget that electronics manufacturing has been the engine of growth for all newly-developed economies. It is projected that the total demand for electronic goods globally will reach $400 billion in 2020. India should be prepared for that. At present, we import 95 per cent of electronics and computer hardware from China. In 2010, we imported goods worth $45 billion. Why don't we learn from the success of Shenzhen, the leading city in China for electronics manufacturing? The way that city has been developed, it is simply a miracle. In 2010, it generated a GDP of $152 billion. Clearly, it can be an excellent lesson for India.

The attention on the electronics sector has to increase. If we don't take the necessary steps now, then in fifteen years our electronics imports burden will become more than that of oil. The rules of the game must change, and they must change immediately. We already have a Semiconductor Policy which can develop this sector. But it needs radical amendments to boost basic research and development by involving academic institutions and synergising the outcomes of such basic R & D with product development by the private sector.

Also, the policy needs to prioritise manufacturing of basic elements in the product cycle. Thus, we should be manufacturing solar cells, rather than just assembling the solar cells imported from China and elsewhere into solar modules. Only then we could become technology leaders, and the economic gains to our nation could be long-lasting as the end product would grow. The government must build the confidence of those who are engaged in manufacturing of such primary elements of the product cycle by giving higher, sustained and timely incentives.

PILLS FOR GROWTH

The government is expected to do its best to provide quality healthcare. We, as a nation, face a serious risk of depleted human capital as chronic hunger, malnutrition, poor hygiene and tropical diseases continue to take a heavy toll on our health. In addition, widespread pollution is threatening to critically weaken our already poor labour productivity forever. The goals of the NRHM are indeed laudable in this context, but as I mentioned earlier, the Mission needs a radical change in its strategic design in order to release the immense energy that the private healthcare sector has in store for public good.

Another critical issue that hasn't changed at all in the last six decades is the pricing of medicines. The Indian pharmaceutical industry is the third largest producer in the world and is poised to grow into a $20 billion behemoth by 2015. But the way multinationals are buying out Indian companies, it doesn't bode too well for the industry and the nation. Certain manufacturers exploit the archaic policies and the drug prescription system to make huge profits that can be anything between 100-3,000 per cent. Such varied pricing and high profit margins make many medicines unaffordable for the common Indian. While there is no denying that a market-based pricing model must remain at the core of the drug policy, the government must encourage wider competition by incentivising drug research and development, building the capacity of smaller players and extending them a level playing field, and making suitable amendments so that doctors and hospitals prescribe drug molecules rather than specific brands. Bihar can be an ideal example to follow. Here every government hospital—from district to primary health centre—has a generic shop run on contractual basis. Only generic medicines are sold here at 50 per cent cost of the market price. Yet, the government manages to make 45 per cent profit.

Another major problem of the health sector is that most hospitals face serious difficulty in getting blood when it is urgently required. A remedy for this would be to provide individuals with a blood bank card, something on the lines of a credit card. So the person who needs blood just has to show the card and get blood immediately. I am trying to introduce this in my constituency, though I have already started it within a small group. One more option can be to record every blood donation in a person's driving licence as credit, which can then be used to donate blood and save lives.

A way to solve the poor doctor-patient ratio in India would be by providing land and financial assistance on public-private partnership basis to anyone who is ready to build a medical college at the district headquarters. This will also make tertiary healthcare available in each district of India. At present, India's state of tertiary healthcare and doctor-patient ratio is poor.

Also, we need to put more effort in population stabilisation. I found it very funny that we are providing ₹1,600 and free transportation for institutional deliveries while ₹500 to those who have tubal ligation or vasectomy. If the subsidies that the government provides to one person are calculated, they would amount to a few million rupees in the person's life. To encourage families to have one child, the government should provide free education at the school of their choice as well as free medical treatment. This would certainly attract families to have only one child. Free school education is possible if it is merged with 25 per cent seats of private schools under the Sarva Shiksha Abhiyan.

CLEAN, GREEN ENERGY

This is going to be the future of the world. India has to get serious about investing in renewable energy sources. It is rather strange that a country which set up the world's first ministry of non-conventional energy resources in the 1980s, has still not explored this sector fully. The potential is immense. India receives abundant sunlight which is the source for solar energy. Wind and biomass are also to be found in plenty. The clean energy sector is pegged at $20 billion annually and has the potential to generate 10 million jobs in India by 2025. That is why it becomes even more essential to develop this sector. Of course, the way we are consuming our non-renewable sources of energy, we need to have alternative sources ready. More importantly, renewable energy is green energy and that's what we need to save the Earth from disaster.

Electrification of villages is a problem that's still not been solved in spite of various schemes launched by the government. The solution, I believe, can be found in West Champaran, my constituency. Nearly 100 villages in the district are using electricity produced from rice husks. The husk is a no-good by-product which is usually discarded. But many rice millers were using this technology to electrify their mills for decades. The idea to use it to light up villages struck two young men, Gyanesh Pandey and Ratnesh Yadav, who eventually set up the Husk Power Systems. The first village to be electrified from its 100 per cent biomass-based power plant was in 2007. Today, more than 25,000 households in over 250 villages use electricity produced from the humble rice husk. This, of course, is a private initiative.

The government, too, can replicate this in other villages across India. It needn't be only rice husks everywhere. The Northeast, for instance, can be lit up using bamboo. The biomass gasification technology can be used with any biomass source with a moisture content of less than 20 per cent. Only minor modifications (e.g. aquatic weeds in fresh water and marine bodies; forest weeds from plantations and protected areas; waste from wood and bamboo-based industries; flowered bamboo areas etc. in case of biomass) are required. Bamboo for power generation is ideal for places where bamboo already grows on a large scale and bamboo processing industries are available. The northeastern states are an excellent example. Bamboo accounts for 12.8 per cent of the total forest cover in India, with the northeast Himalayan region being home to more than 66 per cent of the Indian bamboo genetic resources.

Bamboo plantation is suitable for the clean-cut forestlands, degraded and non-agricultural lands. It is also perhaps the fastest growing plant with some varieties growing at the rate of 5 cm per hour or 1.5 metres a day. Utilisation of this renewable fuel can save vast natural forest resources and fossil fuels such as coal, oil and gas. Also, unlike woody crops, bamboo offers the possibility of annual selective harvesting and removal of about 15-20 per cent of the total stock without damaging the environment and stock productivity. Proper utilisation of bamboo-based sources for electricity generation could spur rural prosperity in the hinterlands—not only in the Northeast where the bamboo landscape is the most dominant but also in the rural areas of south-west and north Bengal, western and northern Odisha, Jharkhand, Chhattisgarh, Madhya Pradesh, Andhra Pradesh and north-eastern Maharashtra.

The other option of electrifying villages as well as urban areas can be through solar power. This is one energy source that we are not tapping into enough. By conservative estimates, the solar potential of India is 70 GW but in reality it could be closer to 500 GW. India gets about 300 sunny days that can help to generate an estimated 5 trillion MW of energy. India's energy demands are increasing by the day. As per the Ministry of Power, India will build up to 316 GW by 2020—from the current installed base of 170 GW. In such a scenario, more schemes and investments in this sector are needed.

Another option is wind power. It is commercially and operationally the most viable energy source. India has made some progress in this area— it has the fifth largest installed wind power capacity in the world. In 2010, India added 2,139 MW of new wind energy installations, a record high for the nation, says a report by Global Wind Energy Council (GWEC). The states with highest wind power concentration are Tamil Nadu, Maharashtra, Gujarat, Rajasthan, Karnataka, Madhya Pradesh and Andhra Pradesh. The world over—especially in 75 countries—wind farms are generating energy from this clean energy source. There is no reason why we can't do the same. In fact, Uttarakhand has great potential which has been finally realised by the government. The Uttarakhand Renewable Energy Development Agency (UREDA) is in the process of setting up a 2.4 MW Grid Interactive Wind Power Generation Project at Bacheli Khal in Tehri Garhwal. Hopefully, more such projects will be seen in other states with wind power.

The Department of Telecom has made it mandatory for all mobile companies to tap into renewable energy sources. The new rule lays down that at least 50 per cent of towers and 20 per cent of urban towers will be powered by hybrid energy sources. This is being done to reduce carbon emissions from use of diesel. I feel this is a significant move as I had raised questions on the subsidies being given to mobile towers for diesel generators.

A group of some twenty-five young MPs from different political parties are members of the Climate Parliament, which works on climate and renewable energy issues. As one of the members, I have moved a proposal to replace diesel-generating sets with renewable energy for supplying power to around 150,000 health centres under NRHM.

I firmly believe that renewable energy can solve the problems of India in many ways—not only could it build energy security by tapping into our diverse resources and reducing our import dependence, but it could also be successfully deployed in areas and sectors which are seriously lagging behind. Rural enterprise, agriculture, food processing, community health, primary schools, rural communications, Panchayati Raj governance etc. are sectors that are energy starved. For these sectors, renewable energy offers new hope, as the centralised fossil-fuel based electricity generation and distribution models have failed to benefit them. To this end, I made comprehensive recommendations for the development of renewable energy in the country as a member of the Estimates Committee in 2011. The committee has recommended increasing the budget of the Ministry of New & Renewable Energy from 0.024 per cent of the Union Budget to at least 1 per cent.

In addition, I have initiated several progressive interventions in the Parliament for the promotion of renewable energy. These include increase in the target for off-grid solar power for rural applications under the National Solar Mission; village mini-grids and allied power infrastructure to tap the decentralised generation of electricity from abundant renewable energy sources, among others.

Politics runs in my blood, quite literally. I have grown up in a family of politicians, with my father, Dr Madan Prasad Jaiswal, being a three-time parliamentarian. It was but natural that I should follow in his footsteps. It was equally natural to pursue a career in medicine after having grown up in a family of medical practitioners. I believe combining the two—medicine and politics—is the best way to serve the people. When I reached Parliament after winning the elections, I realised that I was a nobody. Back in my constituency, I had the trust of the people and was known, but here, at the centre of power, I was just one of the many MPs. That's when I realised that I have to make a difference, not just to my constituency but to the country. As India moves towards becoming a superpower by leaps and bounds, I hope to contribute to its growth.

ಐ೧೩

Index